CHARLES NOBLE

CHARLES NOBLE

Guardian Of
The Soil

Grant MacEwan

Western Producer Prairie Books
Saskatoon, Saskatchewan

Cover design by John Luckhurst/GDL

Western Producer Prairie Book publications are produced
and manufactured in the middle of Western Canada by a
unique publishing venture owned by a group of prairie
farmers who are members of Saskatchewan Wheat Pool.
From the first book published in 1954, a reprint of a serial
originally carried in the weekly newspaper, *The Western
Producer,* to the book before you now, the tradition of
providing enjoyable and informative reading for all Canadians
is continued.

Canadian Cataloguing in Publication Data

MacEwan, Grant, 1902-
   Charles Noble, guardian of the soil

Includes index.
ISBN 0-88833-092-8

1. Noble, Charles, 1873-1957. 2. Farmers - Alberta -
Biography. 3. Alberta - History. I. Title.

S417.N6M325   630'.92'4   C83-091102-2

CONTENTS

PREFACE

Why did I fix upon Charles Noble as an object of research and the subject of this book?

There were various reasons, as might be expected, among them the belief that Canadian agriculture and Canadian agriculturists have together represented a neglected area in historical writing. Agricultural history is both exciting and useful and deserves more attention from writers and readers, whether they hold inherited farm loyalties or not. And the story of farming in any land begins with brave and imaginative men and women.

Noble, quite obviously, was not an average specimen. He would not have been an "average" in any company, and his story is as gripping as it is unusual. At the time the provinces of Saskatchewan and Alberta were being formed, he was still one of thousands of new Canadians struggling to "prove up" on prairie homesteads. Fifteen years later, he was the biggest farm operator in Canada and one of the biggest in the world. But the size of his farming business left him vulnerable and, sure enough, the cruel blows from dry years, heavy debt, and falling prices in the postwar slump laid him low in total bankruptcy.

Noble was down but he refused to stay down, and in a dramatic recovery, he made his second career, still in agriculture, more meaningful and useful than the first.

Certainly one of the reasons for fixing upon Noble as a writing subject was simple admiration for the man. I admired his modesty in a letter written to me on December 29, 1939, in which he discouraged a proposal about writing his biography, saying: "There is really nothing outstanding nor worth mentioning . . . and any account of our work would not be found particularly useful. . . ."

I admired the complete dedication to his chosen vocation and the courage and drive and inventiveness that carried him to fame, not just once but twice. But more than anything, I suppose, I admired his lifelong concept of soil conservation.

The West had its great soil scientists, salaried men who served conscientiously and well, but in sounding warnings about the high cost of carelessness in soil management, nobody was ahead of this unpaid farmer practising and preaching with a missionary zeal. He was one of the first to recognize that cropping practices were reducing soil fibre, depleting reserves of plant food, and inviting erosion.

Some onlookers might have said he was "a nut about soil," but they could never say he was motivated by salary from the public treasury, and nobody could say he was not intensely sincere.

A nation could exhaust its oil and natural gas resources — as Canada was doing with inordinate haste — and survive. But to let soils be blown away or lose their productivity, Noble noted, would be suicidal. Canadian complacency about soils made him sad.

Noble had messages for today's Canadians. The treasure of experience accumulated by every person blessed with a long and an active life is something to be shared. In the light of his ups and downs, his spectacular achievements and inventions, and his dedication to soil conservation, the Noble treasury was particularly rich.

Charles Sherwood Noble, M.B.E., LL.D., was one of the westerners about whom all Canadians should know more.

Again, I declare gratitude to those people to whom I turned, from time to time, for help in the preparation of this work. Members of the Noble family were most helpful and I would mention, especially, Mr. and Mrs. Shirley Noble, Mrs. Alleen Noble Reich, and Mrs. Lillian Noble. Mr. Carlton Stewart, with a long association with Noble Cultivators Limited and an equally long interest in western history, was most cooperative, as were Mrs. Wilma Flitton, Mr. Edward Fraser, and Mr. and Mrs. Percy Woolsey. To all, I express gratitude.

1
A NUT ABOUT
PRAIRIE SOILS

Spring came late to the Canadian foothills, and the mosquitoes were bigger, more numerous, and more savage than ever seen before. Charles Sherwood Noble's adopted village of Claresholm, commanding a restricted view of the multicolored Rockies, would accept the mosquitoes with nothing more than passing complaint but was visibly depressed because of the crippling cattle losses sustained on nearby ranges during the winter just ended. Residents trying to forget the anxieties of the prolonged cold and then the excessive snowfall in April were in a mood to welcome any form of diversion, even something as dull as a free lecture on dry farming, in which most people had not yet discovered an interest.

The provincial Department of Agriculture was sponsoring the meeting, but it was the energetic local farmer and businessman Charlie Noble who was promoting it and promising that it would be a big one. It had now been four years since Iowa-born Noble had filed on the Claresholm homestead, and already his business interests included farming, machinery sales, and real estate. He was an aggressive fellow, but he too, it seemed, had his eccentricities: "He's a smart fellow," the neighbors were saying, "but he's a nut about soils."

Hence the morning trek to the tar-papered Wilton hotel on that June 26, 1907. Homesteaders wearing straw hats and bib-type overalls and townsmen sporting uncomfortable bowler hats and high celluloid collars — the kind that wearers could wash with soap and water without removing them from their necks — crowded into the little hotel. Had the ranchers from back in the hills seen fit to attend, their oversized cowboy headpieces would have added another character to the hat parade. But the rangemen were totally absent because they would not have been at ease in the presence of the more numerous homesteaders.

This shapeless new town, from which the grassy foothills could be seen bounding down from the high west to meet the plains, had witnessed conflict bordering on violence between the grazers and the sodbusters. The former, presuming prior rights on that grassland where they had, until so recently, enjoyed the freedom of open range, resented the settlers who were flocking into the country and fencing quarter sections with the hated barbed wire. Any fencing that would exclude range cattle from good water holes as well as good grazing was bound to be a source of irritation, enough to incite ranchers to anger and occasional acts of vandalism carried out with wire cutters.

The neighboring ranchers, moreover, were still under a spell of shock from the winter losses and could scarcely find the spirit to appear in public. The lingering smell of rotting cow carcasses would not let them forget the most disastrous winter in twenty years. Almost fifty per cent of the ranch cattle had perished. George Lane of the Bar U Ranch could count 25,000 head on his grass in the previous autumn and found only 12,000 alive in the spring.

But anybody with the gift of prophecy or an understanding of ranchers would have known that the industry would recover. Ranchers and farmers in the area might not have been on speaking terms at the time of the Claresholm meeting, but the two groups were about to combine to make the town the leading Alberta shipping point for both wheat and cattle within three years.

Only men attended farm meetings. Women were loath to admit an interest in the vulgar affairs of the barnyard or even the groveling field operations called cultivation. Indeed, there were many farm males who had not yet found more than a most indifferent feeling for soil. Certainly, a dry land farming lecture would never rival a platform debate between the political heavyweights of those years, Frank Oliver from Edmonton and R. B. Bennett from Calgary, in generating public excitement, but any meeting on any subject offered that much desired change from day-to-day work on the homestead or in the shop. Most men getting the message about the free lecture — mainly through the efforts of Charlie Noble — could think of reasons why they should see and hear the speaker, H. W. Campbell, a man gaining fame on both sides of the boundary as "Dustmulch Campbell."

Campbell was a Vermonter who migrated to South Dakota in 1879 and went from there to Nebraska, where he became an international authority on dry farming. The term, which he claimed to have coined, recognized the need for special attention to cultural techniques and moisture conservation on the Great Plains of both the United States and Canada. His teachings, sure enough, seemed to change farming practices in the Midwestern States. Now, officials of the two-year-old Alberta Department of Agriculture thought well enough of Campbell's message to engage him for a tour of sixteen farm lectures starting with Medicine Hat, including Claresholm on this 26th of June, 1907, and ending at Didsbury, all in the southern part of the young province.[1]

The speaker, always fluent and long-winded, did not fail his Claresholm audience, but in the stuffy atmosphere of the hotel meeting place, his evangelical powers were tested. Most of the farmers yawned and some fell asleep in their chairs. Not so the tall man — six feet two inches — with fair hair, a red mustache, and penetrating blue eyes, Charles Noble, sitting at the very center of the front row. He was one of those who came in a straw hat and certainly the one who was mainly responsible for the large attendance. He did not yawn. As keenly alert as a cat watching a bird, the thirty-four-year-old homesteader had not forgotten the drought years and drifting soil and unexplained crop yield variations he had seen in North Dakota. There had to be reasons for everything, and Noble, with the lingering curiosity of an eager scientist, wanted to know what secrets the soils were keeping from him.

At the end of the meeting, as others in the audience were leaving the hotel and Campbell was preparing to drive by democrat to Fort Macleod for an evening meeting, Noble introduced himself and asked questions about soil and cultivation problems that identified him clearly as a serious student of the subjects under discussion. He could tell of having discovered some of the same principles when farming in North Dakota, mainly aids in conserving moisture such as deep plowing, soil compaction, and a surface mulch of loose soil. He could tell about threshing exactly twice as much wheat per acre as his North Dakota neighbors in one dry year. The soil was the same but cultivation made the difference.

Campbell was impressed, and as he continued to pack away

his notes and papers, a lasting friendship between the two men possessing similar concerns about soil was born.

Campbell seemed to reinforce Noble's hopes and substantiate his fears, making this meeting an unofficial induction into the unorganized fraternity of soil workers for the younger man. Noble did not use a speaker's platform in the manner of Campbell at that time, but when the latter returned for a repeat tour in southern Alberta one year later, he found Noble speaking out more boldly about soil management and conservation. It was indeed a surprising theme in a new district where soils were still too fresh to awaken fears in any except the most sensitive observers. Noble was, by the keenness of his observations or his intuition, one of the first to sense the dangers in careless field practices such as burning stubble and allowing precious soil moisture to escape, and also in the haphazard occupation of western lands which for reasons of low average precipitation or low fertility should not have been opened for homesteading in the first place. Like one who was ahead of his time, he was talking about soil erosion before it was in evidence and depletion before there was depletion. He was even using his own farm fields for simple crop experiments before the first dominion experimental station was in operation in Alberta.

Men on the frontier took a dubious view of farm professors and academics, but Noble, with only a public school education, was not likely to be confused with the learned ones. He proved that a person could be a great without being an academic. As time was to prove, he possessed the native imagination to become a research worker, an agricultural inventor, and an agricultural leader, with soil as his basic interest and soil as his passion.

When he sat at "Dustmulch Campbell's" meetings or when he strode without shoes behind his first walking plow in the homestead years, he didn't look much different from 10,000 others coming annually to find free land in the Canadian West, and he did not try to appear any different. There was not the slightest outward reason to suspect that this humble but busy man would someday be Canada's biggest farm operator with assets placing him in the millionaire category. Nor would anybody have guessed that his faith in prairie soils and dedication to the practical tasks of rescuing and preserving them would bring some of the country's highest honors, like the award of M.B.E. — Member of the Order of the British Empire, 1943 — an honorary doctor's degree from the University of Alberta, and elevation to the Agricultural Hall of Fame in his province. The fact, whether recognized in the early years or not, was that with his imagination, business courage, and stamina to match his big frame, this man was destined to stand out in the ranks of his fellows like a sunflower growing in a potato patch.

If Charles Noble had entered the army, he would have retired as a general. If he had taken to politics, his resolve and determination would have made him a candidate for the office of prime minister. But he had no desire to be a soldier or a politician; he wanted to be the biggest and most progressive dry land farmer and he was not one to compromise.

His farm holdings, which in 1918 consisted of fifty-six sections, were enough to make him Canada's biggest farm operator and one of the biggest in the world. And to dispel any doubt about the quality of his massive operations, leaders and students could accept the judgment of the Honorable Duncan Marshall when he was Alberta's minister of agriculture between 1909 and 1921. The minister declared publicly that Charles Noble was "the best tiller of soil in semi-arid districts."[2]

But being the biggest and the best gave no guarantee of uninterrupted success, especially when so much of farm fortune depended upon the whims of weather and markets. Reverses were inevitable and Noble's setbacks were as massive as his successes. The man who had 33,000 acres of farm land — nearly all in cultivation — and over two million dollars in assets one day was reduced to little more than his household furniture the next. If he had decided to quit farming after that crushing bankruptcy, nobody would have been surprised or blamed him.

Noble needed a soldier's fighting tenacity and had it. He refused to surrender further. The reverses revealed a philosophical trait in his nature. It was his determined view that setbacks could be and should be turned to advantage, including economic advantage. The experiences of a failure should be used to prevent a recurrence of the same. Yesterday's experiences — good or bad — are at once history, and history has always been mankind's best teacher, whether accorded a hearing or not.

Noble's fortunes fluctuated dramatically, but still his affection for the soil and dedication to it did not waver. Soil was his obsession, always had been it seemed. His brother told facetiously that Charlie was found to have loam under his fingernails at birth. However that may be, there was proof of correspondents wishing to communicate with Charles S. Noble, writing to "Mr. Charles Soil Noble."

His views about cultural practices shifted with the passing years, naturally, but his searching curiosity did not change. At first he agreed with Angus MacKay's ideas about summer-fallowing and the H. W. Campbell teachings about dry farming cultivation. In both cases the theories were good in their time, but as the "top six inches" lost native fibre and hence stability, cultural methods had to change. There could be no rest for a serious student of soils.

Summerfallowing, seen as a necessity in dry land farming, offered a good example. Over much of the Great Plains, an average season's rainfall was not enough to provide for a fair crop return every year. It was sufficient to give a good crop every second year, provided proper methods were employed to prevent needless losses of the moisture. Hence the practice of summerfallowing as demonstrated accidentally at Indian Head in 1885 and 1886. That district at the eastern edge of the Palliser Triangle was already the home of some of the most progressive farmers on the frontier, men like Major William Bell of the famous Bell Farm; Angus MacKay, who was to become the first superintendent of the Indian Head Experimental Farm; and W. R. Motherwell, who became Saskatchewan's first Minister of Agriculture and later one of Canada's greatest ministers of agriculture.

When rebellion trouble erupted along the South Saskatchewan River south of Prince Albert in 1885 and troops were being rushed with fire engine speed from the East, farmers near the Canadian Pacific Railroad station of Troy heard the call for horse teams with wagons and drivers for transport service to the fighting zone. Providing work horses to move military supplies was a patriotic duty; it was also more profitable than farming. Consequently, farm operations near Troy and Indian Head suffered, and men like MacKay were able to do little more than keep the weeds down on their crop land during that summer.

The loss of crop in rebellion year appeared unfortunate, but it brought good returns in the next year. Drought accounted for crop failure nearly everywhere in the Indian Head area except on the MacKay and Bell land which, during the fallow year, had been given an opportunity to accumulate a reserve of moisture. On the MacKay farm the summerfallowed land yielded twenty-six bushels of wheat per acre, and homesteaders came for miles to see for themselves.[3]

The principle of summerfallow, actually discovered in the ancient world, was now rediscovered in the Canadian West and adopted as a necessary device in semiarid regions. But to be effective, MacKay and then Noble said, all moisture-consuming weeds had to be kept down throughout the fallow year.

In due course, Campbell came along to share his observations about the right and wrong ways to perform the summer-fallowing operation. His advice sounded reasonable. First, as he explained, the land to be fallowed must be harrowed in the autumn to destroy the offending weeds, then plowed at least six or seven inches deep in the spring to loosen subsoil and let water penetrate from the surface. Crucial in Campbell's theory was a subsoil packing followed by frequent shallow cultivations to insure a blanket of loose soil or "dust mulch" on the surface to break the capillary rise of moisture from the subsoil, thereby preventing evaporation.

"Harrow after every rain," Campbell would instruct, emphasizing the importance of keeping the blanket or mulch loose and effective.[4] That was fine until about 1911, when southern Alberta was seeing dust storms, with the dust mulch summer-fallows being the first victims. Noble was a leader in declaring that cultural methods had to be changed. He had seen soil drifting in the western states and knew it could be ruinous. He was one of the first to condemn the dust mulch or clean summerfallow and conferred with W. H. Fairfield and other workers at the Lethbridge Experimental Station. He talked to his neighbors, Arie Koole and brothers at Monarch, men who later adopted and demonstrated the soil-saving device of strip farming. The inquisitive fellow then travelled to various experimental stations in the northwestern states to learn what was being done to check wind erosion, especially on summer-fallows prepared by MacKay's and Campbell's methods. At the same time, Noble was conducting his own tests with new machines and new techniques which, hopefully, would not only save moisture but actually save soil.

Farming methods are not changed in a hurry, but when the faulty dust mulch or clean summerfallow was giving place to the untidy but useful trash cover and the users of the conventional plows were turning away from them, Noble was among the leaders. Research workers from across the West and some from south of the border were coming to Noble's Nobleford to observe the innovations on the big farm.

Dr. Asael Palmer, with a long association at the Lethbridge Experimental Station, wrote that: "The Nobleford, Monarch,

Barons district became the first in Western Canada and perhaps in the world to abandon the plow and adopt plowless trash-cover fallowing completely. The result was that during the 'dirty thirties,' there was practically no drifting in those areas."[5]

When new and totally different cultivating machines were needed to protect the fields from destroying winds, the inventive genius of Charles Noble was one of those that succeeded. The Noble Blade Cultivator, although extremely simple in construction, proved to be a maker of farm history and a monument to its creator.

More than ever, soil conservation was becoming an obsession, and Noble was taking his place with the great teachers and research workers such as his friends H. W. Campbell, Dr. W. H. Fairfield, Dr. Asael Palmer, L. B. Thomson, Gordon Taggart, Grant Denike, D. G. Mathews, and others in government and university services.

There were, however, some important points of difference between Charles Noble and those other well known dry land figures; they were public servants, paid and supported by the public treasury, while he was a farmer acting like a public servant but paying his own way. In rendering private citizen service in the interest of better understanding of dry land soils and the people who must depend upon them, Charles Noble stood alone and earned the nation's applause.

Even in the United States, workers in soil and water conservation research joined to praise Charles Noble. F. L. Duley of the United States Department of Agriculture Research Branch, located at the College of Agriculture at Lincoln, Nebraska, would write proudly in 1956: "We have kept in touch with Mr. Noble for nearly 20 years. He has made frequent visits here to observe the results and methods of our experiments ... and I have visited his farm and plant in Alberta. We have considered him our most reliable and active co-operator. Just before receiving your letter I had written him for suggestions and advice concerning new research work on wind erosion control which we are starting in Western Nebraska. ..."

And then the highly regarded American scientist added a personal tribute, saying: "We have always considered Mr. Noble one of the finest gentlemen we have ever known."[6]

It was the sort of compliment which should have reached more Canadian ears and left Canadians with the wish to know more about one of their supermen in agriculture.

He made no secret of his own assessment of farming as a

career. His own experience, considering setbacks as well as triumphs, had been richly worthwhile, he said. Standing in a field of waving wheat and facing the distant Rockies, he challenged a group of visiting boys. The display of attention showed that the young visitors knew they were in the presence of a leader of men. He told them that if they hoped to find easy wealth or make fortunes without struggles and headaches, they should not choose farming. But if they possessed the will and courage to accept some of Canada's biggest challenges, like producing food without doing injury to the soil, they could find rewarding places in agriculture. For his part, he confessed solemnly that if he had six lives to live, he would hope to be a dry land farmer in western Canada six times.

The size of his farming operations made Charles Noble an interesting Canadian; his almost religious zeal for soil and its care made him a great Canadian.

2
CHARLIE WILL MAKE HIS MARK IN THE WORLD

Hubert and Jemima Noble of State Center, where the corn grew tall in Iowa, did not have much of this world's goods about which to boast. They and members of their big family knew all about the inconvenience of poverty. Their son Charles told about carrying his shoes under his arm when walking to the country school in his home district. By so doing, he could enjoy the prestige of shoes on his feet during school hours without imposing needless wear and tear on them when walking to and from home.

For the struggling parents, their principal wealth and luxuries were in their eight children, of whom Charles was the second son. The boys and girls might be short of good clothes and the Noble pantry might be close to depletion at times, but they were healthy. If the ultimate record of their successes and achievements were taken as an indication, the Nobles' humble home was indeed a good one.

The mother, Jemima Sherwood before she was married, possessed such fortitude that she would not allow the handicap of partial invalidism for most of her years to prevent the realization of an extremely active, although short, career. She taught school before she was married and then spent her remaining years raising children, patching and darning small garments, and struggling to satisfy childhood appetites. Her dream was of a better life for her family and herself, but she did not live long enough to see it come true.

Jemima's husband, Hubert, was a God-fearing, law-abiding citizen, but with no special skills and less enterprise than his wife, he earned only enough in wages to buy the bare minimum in needed food and clothing. As his children grew older, they never ceased to marvel that their father's monthly wage of fifteen dollars during the winter when he clerked in a local store could be stretched to pay for even the necessities.

They might be constantly close to the poverty line, but Hubert and Jemima Noble were conscientious people, regular churchgoers who were proud of their children and, like most Americans, proudly interested in their ancestral connections even though some individuals were remembered more for their peculiarities than for their success or useful performance. Charlie often heard his elders talking about grandparents and certain of the great-grandparents, keeping their memory alive while admitting that not all were paragons of industry or virtue. The list inevitably included sinners as well as saints.

The boy's grandfather, William Noble, was regarded as one of the more saintly of the ancestors, presuming, of course, that a man who had been a successful horse trader could qualify for contention at all. He had served with the Union side in the Civil War, having run away from home at the age of seventeen and become a drummer boy in uniform. But he was a good farmer, with straight furrows and sturdy rail fences, and it was his farming skill coupled with the ownership of a fine barn and the ability to lead in prayer that attracted Tryphena Sedgwick, who became his wife and the grandmother who helped to care for Charlie's brothers and sisters when their mother died. Tryphena Noble's specialty was taking in orphans and giving them a home and doses of castor oil and mother's love as needed. The good woman had helped so many children that she lost count and could only estimate the numbers.

That grandmother was one of thirteen children born to Parker Sedgwick and his wife in New York State. And old Parker, who traced to Mayflower stock, was no less positive about everything he did or did not do. He was one of those eccentrics at whom every family liked to be able to point and laugh. It was an enjoyment that seemed to grow better as the ancestral subjects receded into antiquity.

Hiding in the withered branches of every family tree were some of these "rare birds" who during their lives brought more embarrassment than satisfaction and failed to win popularity until a couple of generations after their deaths. They could be drifters, ne'er-do-wells, or outright scoundrels who were lucky to be out of jail. But with the passing of time their sins were forgiven, and they were likely to be elevated to a place reserved for heroes. The name of some Scottish sheep stealer about whom contemporary kinsmen would not speak above a whisper was likely, in time, to become a family relic whose brigandage could be recounted with boastful chuckles.

Parker Sedgwick was not a wicked man by any stretch of imagination, but by his quaint and idle ways, spending most of his hours at reading, he was an exasperating fellow, especially for his wife, until she could stand it no longer and threatened the use of force to convert him to activity. He had better think about becoming a breadwinner for a change, she told him while performing a fancy juggling act with a rolling pin. "If you must spend all your time reading," she proposed in a more conciliatory tone, "why don't you read up on something useful and apply it to making grocery money for your family?"

Parker Sedgwick took the hint seriously. Just as he had been an idler — the local character who knew the answer to everything except making a living — he now took enthusiastically to the study of medicine. After reading everything available on the subject, he wrote a book on home treatment of the sick and became the self-made authority whose advice was sought throughout the state of New York and later Illinois.[1]

One point should have been made very clear to Charles Sherwood Noble: that individuality in pronounced form had been one of the recurring fruits from his family tree. And as others could judge, the tree was still productive.

Charlie's birth was at State Center on May 16, 1873 — seven days before the government bill to authorize the formation of the North West Mounted Police was passed in the Canadian House of Commons.

Perhaps it is not correct that he had loam under his fingernails when he was born, but it was unmistakably clear before long that he would not play on the floor or grass if he could get into the garden soil. His good mother grew tired of trying to stop him from putting soil into his mouth and finally concluded that it was doing him no harm. When his natural love of soil was noted in later years, he could explain that he had eaten more than his share of it.

His mother's fine strength of character became clear, and Charlie and his brothers and sisters were beneficiaries. She was a firm disciplinarian and believed in administering appropriate punishment on bare bottoms. Her principles and convictions demanded strict Sabbath observance, and nobody in the family argued. Preparation for the day of rest began on Saturday night and called for the performance of as many Sunday chores as could be done in advance. It might also include a Saturday night preparatory class for Sunday school, conducted at the kitchen table.

Thinking of temporal needs as well as spiritual, it was Mother Noble's constant hope that her children would become self-reliant people. She wanted them to have good business sense. There was nothing evil about recognizing a good bargain. In fact, the greater sin might be in ignoring a bargain. To her satisfaction, Charlie was showing signs of business awareness at a tender age. According to his older brother, Charlie at five years of age was visiting a neighboring farm when he frightened a setting hen from her nest, leaving thirteen eggs exposed. That the hen had just laid all these eggs at the same time was a reasonable conclusion for the child, and he hastened home to tell his mother that it was time she invested in a good hen which would far outscore the ordinary hens that never did better than an egg a day.

The first real business enterprise came a short time later when Charlie, cooperating with his mother, was taking radishes, carrots, beets, and cucumbers from her garden and peddling them in the neighborhood. Most of the returns went into Mrs. Noble's ever-depleted grocery fund, and a few cents went into Charlie's savings, to grow until he had enough to buy his own vegetable seeds.

The boy was eight years old when his enterprising and loving mother died. It was a day of gloom and tragedy for the children — all under twelve years of age — and no less a catastrophe for Hubert Noble, who knew he could not bring proper parental attention to his children while working to buy food for them. It was inevitable that some of the children would have to be placed in the homes of friends and neighbors. Charlie was already conspicuously useful around a farmyard, and a neighbor offered to take him to perform farm chores in return for board and lodging and a chance to attend school.

The farm chores were done well although school attendance suffered. Before long, the boy was finding extra jobs such as selling papers, delivering milk, and hoeing gardens. And while most boys were attending baseball games to play or watch, he attended to sell peanuts. His mother would have been pleased with his display of enterprise and the dispatch with which he recognized an opportunity or a bargain. The character and shape of the man he would become was appearing. He was big for his age and strong. He would have been a good baseball player had he not been so fully engaged in selling peanuts. Athletic capabilities were never really tested beyond riding horseback. But as a horseman, young Charlie was one of the best, and his demonstrated ability extended even to outlaw horses.

It was increasingly difficult to find the time to attend school, and at the age of fifteen he knew he had to depend upon himself alone for his living. Schooling ended abruptly at grade eight, and Charlie Noble was at once an adult doing an adult's work. At first he was a farm laborer for ten dollars a month and his board. From each month's payment he saved eight dollars, and at the end of a year he had enough cash for the purchase of two old horses and a wagon.

Still not out of his teens, the tall, eager, blue-eyed kid was using his aged horses to perform dray work on the streets of State Center, hauling coal, lumber, hay, or furniture. The returns were better by far than those obtained by farm workers, and he could afford to trade the old horses for a younger and better team, leading an approving uncle to say, "Charlie will make his mark in the world."

When the horses ended their work day and retired to their stable stalls to rest, the energetic youth continued at other enterprises, often carpentry work at which he was soon proficient. There was satisfaction as well as profit in woodwork, and the bright lad was soon telling seasoned carpenters of easier and better ways of cutting rafters. It was an initial expression of a talent for invention that was to serve him well in Canadian agriculture.

At the age of nineteen, having taken a contract to rebuild a barn that was flattened by a tornado, he was on the verge of getting into the building trade as a contractor. Had he pursued the business of building, he would have gone to the top in his profession, but a person can't do everything. It was work in the familiar field of farming that tugged most strongly at the strings of his heart.

In the autumn of his nineteenth year, Charlie Noble travelled into the northern part of his state to take advantage of the "good wages" being paid for threshing help. The dollar and a quarter a day was matched, of course, by the daylight-to-darkness threshing hours fixed by the tireless steam engine driving the threshing separator.

It was young Noble's first experience with steam power and he was fascinated, so fascinated that before the end of the threshing season, he and the engineer became partners in an undertaking to buy the steamer and thresher with promissory notes. Unfortunately, the partner proved unfaithful to his obligation and withdrew, leaving Charlie alone with the problem of paying the debt. As one who did not smoke or drink, he was able to save all of his $1.25 per day wages, but meeting the promised payments was still not easy.

Thus Charlie Noble was introduced to the steam tractor operator's problems of all night repair jobs, broken bridges, rebellious work crews, and weekend tasks cleaning boiler flues. But the new worries were not without rewards; they gave him a working knowledge of steam power that he would never have gained if his partner in the purchase had not deserted him.

Noble had now reached maturity. He was old enough to vote, old enough to homestead, and old enough to be counted among the eligible bachelors in the farming district. He could break bad horses, pitch hay with the strongest workers, husk one hundred bushels of corn per day, and, having spent several seasons at threshing where smoking was prohibited and workmen felt compelled to chew tobacco, it was difficult to escape learning to do that too. The venture into the northeastern part of his state left him thinking of still more remote opportunities, and he was now feeling that urge which overtakes every young man, to break clear away — to be like Abraham of old and journey to "a far country."

Quarter section homesteads were still obtainable in parts of the American northwest, and North Dakota was the most popular frontier, attracting both Americans and eastern Canadians. But a strong counterattraction appeared suddenly. The first rumors of rich gold strikes were coming out of the Canadian Klondike, and Charlie Noble was one of the many robust young Americans sensing the lure. The most fearless ones were going. The Sherwood spirit of adventure told him to join the growing rush into the distant and unfriendly Yukon while his Noble sense of restraint and conservatism cautioned him to stay with the soil.

Instead of following the crowd to Skagway on the Alaskan coast and proceeding from there on the long and dangerous journey inland, he found himself travelling on the Great Northern Railway into the district of Devil's Lake in northeastern North Dakota. It was semiarid prairie country, less than a hundred miles from the Canadian boundary and roughly south of the Manitoba city of Brandon. The Indians called the lake Minnewaukan or Spirit Water, and the town of Devil's Lake grew up beside it.

Noble had no specific location in mind but stepped off the train at nearby Knox, mainly because most land seekers were passing it by. The native grass looked nutritious, and the soil had a good brown color. The young man selected a homestead quarter a couple of miles from the village and filed on it with every intention of farming it in earnest. He lost no time in buying three horses and a walking plow, then hauling lumber for a stable to shelter his horses and a shack for himself.

His intentions were the best but not good enough to deflect the misfortunes soon to strike. If he had been superstitious, he would have interpreted his troubles as warning signs. Even before he plowed his first furrow on the new quarter, a bolt of lightning in the course of a summer storm killed his three horses and left his stable, harness, and store of feed in ashes. Only his cabin escaped.

Somebody suggested that the shack remained because it was too small to be a good target even for lightning. But it was big enough to serve the essential purposes for a man who did not expect to use it except at mealtime and sleeping hours. It was twelve feet long and eight feet wide, and with a single bed and table and chairs in place, there was about as much remaining floor space for human movement as would be found in a wagon box loaded with a half a dozen pigs for market. But exercising typical ingenuity, Noble attached his bed by means of hinges to one wall and his table by hinges to the opposite wall. When both bed and table were down and in serviceable position, the bed would serve as a seat for the table, and when both were turned up against the walls, the bachelor occupant could walk the length of the cabin and even sweep the floor if he felt constrained to take such extreme measures. After all, it wasn't every homesteader who owned a broom.

Following the loss of his first horses, Noble promptly invested in a replacement team and harness, using his credit to make settlement. He hitched to his walking plow, hoping to get as much breaking as possible done before the middle of July, then spent the balance of the summer and autumn discing and backsetting and harrowing the ground, convinced that most farmers were not getting the returns for which they hoped because of insufficient cultivation. One of his neighbors who had been watching with childish disbelief mustered the courage to warn him that if he did any more cultivating, he would "wear the land out."

At the end of the first crop year, the wisdom of Noble's policies became clear. It was a dry year in that part of North Dakota, and most crops in the Devil's Lake area were bordering on failure. Noble's crop was the district exception, averaging thirty bushels of wheat per acre on his relatively small fields of thoroughly prepared land.

Noble was determined to prove up on the homestead and obtain title to it, but he changed his mind about spending all his time on the place. Men with the skills of a carpenter were needed, and wages could be used most appropriately for the purchase of machinery and more horses. An able man should not be idle. His mother would have agreed.

Again, he acquired a steam engine and threshing machine for custom work, again ignoring the warnings of cautious neighbors that: "the surest road to bankruptcy is the one travelled by owners of studhorses and steam engines." But instead of going broke, Noble paid for the threshing outfit in two or three autumn seasons.

Friends said he was by nature a horse trader, living up to the traditions of his mother's family, the Sherwoods, and Grandfather William Noble. During his second or third winter on the Knox farm, according to a brother, Charlie made a profit of $1,000 on two carloads of horses brought to the district and sold to the settlers who seemed to be constantly short of field power.

He did not overlook the case for specializing in the horse trade. It was a business which commonly showed big "book profits," but the extent of "bad debts" made it discouraging. It seemed impossible to sell farm horses in the pioneer years without taking lien notes, and every dealer discovered the hopelessness of collecting on liens after the horses in question were dead.

Noble proved that he could be a successful salesman, and he might have been one of those who managed to become rich in the horse business. But it was his own conclusion that selling any goods would not satisfy his longing to be working close to the good earth, whether it was profitable or not.

Perhaps there was some truth in the story about loam under his fingernails at birth.

He had not yet tasted all the morsels of good fortune and misfortune that the Knox district held for him. His most painful misfortune and the most costly in loss of time was when he fell down the farm well he was digging and suffered a broken leg. He would never forget the awful struggle of trying to climb out of a well unaided while the fractured limb dangled and inflicted its own kind of torture.

But it was while he was convalescing that a Canadian girl entered his life and changed the direction of his farming career. She was Margaret Fraser, sister of Rev. Simon Fraser, the young minister who had come to occupy the Presbyterian charge at Knox. He had already made many calls at the tiny homestead shack and found the fresh biscuits and meals of Noble's making contradicting the culinary reputation with which homestead bachelors were normally tagged.

Fraser, in serving the church, had been in the districts of Fort Macleod, Pincher Creek, and Claresholm in the Canadian Territories and believed that the Claresholm district offered the best opportunities for farming. Moreover, Ontario-born Fraser had a sister who for reasons of change, was thinking about applying for a teaching position in the schools of North Dakota. With luck, she would stay at the church manse.

Miss Margaret may or may not have considered the inescapable popularity that a female teacher — almost any female teacher — would experience in a homestead district where ninety per cent of the residents were bachelors and where an unattached girl could expect at least one proposal of marriage per month from the time of her arrival.

Margaret Fraser's application for a teaching position was accepted, and she came to the Leeds district. She was brown-haired, dark-eyed, comely, and kind, and all masculine attention was upon her, including that of the manly and enterprising Charles Noble, who was by this time one of the most successful homesteaders in the district. From the outset, Charlie liked Margaret and Margaret liked Charlie — and Simon Fraser approved. Recovery from the broken leg seemed more rapid, and if there was anything to produce surprise, it was that Charlie had time for some courting.

It was increasingly evident that this romance was leading to the altar, but Charlie had admitted to both Margaret and her brother that he was not convinced that he should become permanently attached to the Knox farm. What he had heard about Oregon made him curious, and he invited the opinions of his friends.

The Presbyterian minister's advice was to enquire about farming opportunites in Canada's North West Territories, and Margaret admitted that she would prefer to live permanently in her native land. Charlie was listening attentively, and then, late in 1901, he met a Devil's Lake man Ole J. Amundsen with a nice thick Norwegian accent, who had just returned from the Canadian Northwest and was already talking like a real estate supersalesman, especially about a village called Claresholm where he had made some speculative land purchases. He advised Noble to visit that part with good soil, chinook winds, and magnificent scenery.

Margaret agreed with Ole's advice, and after Charlie's crop was seeded in 1902, he set out to make his own assessment of this place known as Claresholm.

3
SOIL AND SCENERY IN THE CANADIAN NORTHWEST

Claresholm as Charlie Noble saw it in 1902 had an awkwardness about it, making him think of an old cowboy being forced to walk or a newborn foal struggling to stand on its wobbly legs. An unpainted elevator stood alone to break the skyline and looked down paternally at the lowly stockyard built at the track side, mainly to accommodate the shipping needs of the big ranch herds in the nearby foothills. If judged by the amount of lumber used in making it, the stockyard was the biggest structure in the village and probably the most important.

Although this track-side community was neither large nor handsome, it was the shipping point for some of the biggest ranches in the Northwest and had been, until this time, regarded as a ranch land center. Not far away was the New Oxley Ranch operated by an English company and stocked with 8,000 cattle. A little farther removed was the Walrond, also backed by English capitalists, where even the herd bulls were said to bellow with a refined Oxford accent. And scarcely less prominent was the Glengary Ranch owned by railroad magnets Mackenzie and Mann and managed by A. B. McDonald, who was the current president of the Western Stock Growers' Association. Foothills herds driven to the stockyards at Claresholm accounted for some of the most distinct trails leading to the village.

The earliest residents in the area were squatters with

interests in buffalo hunting and whiskey trading, among them Henry Kountz, who built a cabin soon after 1870. The place had a loading platform and a name from 1891 when the railroad was built, but there was not much homestead activity until 1902 when the surrounding soil began to attract settlers from the western states. As for the attractive name, it was taken from that of Clare Niblock, daughter of John Niblock, superintendent of the local division of the CPR.

The village was still unincorporated when Charlie Noble saw it on this initial visit. The shacks and homes and outdoor toilets were scattered like heavy specks of pepper from a giant shaker and did nothing to improve the landscape. Somewhere in the building conglomerate were a general store owned by Fisher and Ross, a post office, and a hotel, but it was not easy to tell which were places of business and which were residences.

Travelling by train, Noble came by way of Calgary and paused there long enough to enlarge his knowledge of nearby homestead opportunities. Didsbury, Olds, and Bowden districts were especially popular at the time, and Noble inspected them, then went south to Nanton and Claresholm. At the latter place he found one familiar face, that of Ole J. Amundsen from Devil's Lake, North Dakota, who was about to start in the real estate business. He was bubbling with enthusiasm and had already purchased a big piece of town site on the west side of the railway tracks and was in the process of buying the section of land adjacent to the village on the east.

Ole Amundsen was a cousin of the celebrated polar explorer Roald Amundsen. Both of these Amundsens were born at Christiana, Norway, although Ole left home to settle in Wisconsin before Roald entered upon his career of exploration.

Ole Amundsen's enterprise was exactly what Claresholm needed. He became land agent for the Calgary and Edmonton Railway Company and the CPR and then used his North Dakota connections to attract midwestern land purchasers. At midsummer in 1902, he brought a party of twenty-five North Dakota farmers — some of them acquaintances of Charlie Noble — to inspect Claresholm land. It was the first large group to come to see and buy. He was reported to have sold twenty-one sections to his North Dakota friends in half a day, much to the distress of nearby ranchers.

For the next six months, Ole Amundsen's land sales averaged four sections per week, making him a force in the development of the town and settlement of the surrounding area. His enthusiasm was infectious, and his cheerful exaggeration was not held against him. When he displayed pictures of workmen on his own farm toiling outdoors in January in their shirt sleeves, most viewers grinned and decided that he had a better climate on his farm than on the places around him. Likewise his report that his men and teams were performing field work — meaning plowing and cultivating — in every month except March, 1904, for a period of twenty-four consecutive months brought more laughter than anger or annoyance.[1]

Among the North Dakota people buying at the time of Charlie Noble's first visit to Claresholm was James McKinney, whose wife, Louise Crummy McKinney, became a national leader in the temperance movement. She was the first woman to be elected to the legislature of Alberta — the first woman in the British Empire to occupy a seat in a legislature. Later, when their respective farms were only about seven miles apart, the McKinneys and Nobles were close friends and saw one another often.[2]

Charlie Noble was an impressed spectator of Amundsen's sensational land sales but was not yet ready to make that crucial decision which should not be made in a hurry, certainly not without conferring with the person who would be sharing his future. He was impressed favorably by the good stands of grass reaching to the horizons on all sides, the deep and rich soil being exposed by new plows, and the exquisite Rocky Mountain scenery visible from Claresholm. At the same time, he was impressed unfavorably by the mudholes seen on the trails and the shabby country villages giving the impression of boasting of their outdoor toilets leaning like the Tower of Pisa. Before buying or homesteading, he would report all these observations to the Canadian girl, Margaret Fraser, teaching school at Leeds and waiting for his reactions. After all, if they were to be married, she had an equal interest in Charlie's next move.

After returning to Dakota and telling Margaret all about his trip, they agreed that plans should be made to move to a new frontier the following spring, probably to Ole Amundsen's Claresholm. Accordingly, Charlie offered his Knox farm for sale and proceeded to sell all horses and equipment except what could be transported in one car of settler's effects.

But before the end of the winter, Charlie's younger brother Will, a civil engineer in the state of Washington, wrote to invite and advise him to choose that area rather than Canada for his next farming venture. He'd find the climate more agreeable and the opportunities more numerous, Will argued. There was everything to be gained by choosing Washington.

Charlie had confidence in Will's judgment, even though the brother had never seen the Canadian countryside under consideration. Margaret was secretly disappointed but believed she could be happy with a home in Washington and was ready to leave the final decision to Charlie. Late in March, Charles Noble loaded his remaining work horses and equipment on a railroad freight car and billed to Windsor in the central part of Washington, just as his educated brother had advised.

The reception in Washington State is best described by Mr. Noble's son Shirley F. Noble: "Arriving in the early morning at the tiny settlement of Windsor, just west of the present town of Quincy, the rising sun disclosed an unpleasant prospect. A light colored soil showed through the straggly patches of thin bunch grass. Dusty wagon trails cut deep and each light breeze raised whirling eddies of dust. This was not for him, for he had not forgotten the lush pasture of the Claresholm foothill country."[3]

Now what? Mr. Noble made his decision instantly, as he made most business decisions. He would sell the horses and machinery and continue right on to western Canada as an immigrant land seeker, as thousands of others were doing. This, he was convinced, was what Margaret Fraser was secretly hoping he would do anyway.

Noble's stay in Washington was short. Leaving the contents of his carload of settler's effects for his brother to sell, he hurriedly took a train to Claresholm, North West Territories, Canada, taking nothing with him except the contents of a small, collapsible leather bag and his lean but strong body.

He wrote to Margaret to explain the sudden change of plans and assured her he would be communicating again just as soon as he knew where he would locate.

Charlie Noble might have concluded from events during his next few weeks in Canada that Nature was trying to discourage him or make his initiation as rough as possible. This time, his train journey to the Canadian prairies would be by way of the Crow's Nest Pass, but he was thoroughly shocked to find his rail route blocked by the tragic Frank Slide which saw a seventy-million-ton chunk of limestone rock falling off Turtle Mountain at 4 a.m. on April 29. The lives of sixty-six men, women, and children were lost — including Mr. and Mrs. Vanduson and their two children who were well known at Claresholm. Being present at the scene a few days after the terrible catastrophe left Charlie Noble dazed. Rock debris was piled to a depth of a hundred feet in the valley where a village had existed, and the smell of death filled the air. All transportation was brutally disrupted, of course, and a long delay for train passengers was inevitable. Finally, Noble and other eastbound passengers were able to leave one stranded train on the west side of the slide and walk around the new mountain of fractured rocks to board another waiting train at the east end of the disaster zone.

The next bad news in this troubled month of May was about unusual spring flooding in various parts of the Alberta area, some of it washing out railway bridges and further delaying Noble's arrival at Claresholm. Many riverside residents in the general area were forced to flee.

What next? As if the forces of Nature were still angry about something, there was the memorable May storm about which ranchers and farmers never ceased to talk and which coincided with Noble's return to Claresholm. Thousands of cattle and sheep perished.

The vicious blizzard began mildly with rain on the 12th of May and rural people were saying, "The moisture will do no harm." But the rain turned to snow, and when Charlie Noble could have been celebrating his thirtieth birthday on May 16, the country was still in the icy grip of the blizzard. For four long days the snow coming in on frosty northwest winds created conditions which neither man nor beast cared to face. Cattle drifted pathetically with the gale, some of them to be found fifty miles from their home range. Hundreds of them ended in death piles in coulees and fence corners. One rancher "Uncle Tony" Day counted 2,000 of his Turkeytrack cattle frozen to death.

They were a gloomy few weeks, and Charlie was glad that Margaret was not present to see the rebellion of which the country was capable. But settlers continued to flock into the country. The seven carloads of settlers' effects unloaded at Claresholm in the last week of May were indicative of the influx.[4] This was the trend that was making the year ending on June 30, 1903, a record one for homestead entries in the Canadian Northwest — 31,002 filings which would be more than twice as many as in the previous year.

And now, after the volatile forces of Nature appeared to have spent all their bad temper, they turned sweet again, and the foothills and plains displayed their usual springtime charm. It was enough to make a young man's thoughts turn to love and homesteads. Charlie was thinking of both, and having confirmed his faith in Claresholm, he at once began searching for a cabin or cottage that he could rent and a quarter section on which he could file.

He was very conscious of the changing village scene. The lone grain elevator was getting a companion, and the number of general stores had doubled since his visit of the previous year from one store to two. William Moffat, who came in 1902 to open a lumberyard and found business so brisk that he did not need a sales yard because he could sell right off the cars as fast as he could get supplies, was now adopting a yard with an office. A second hotel was being constructed, and Olegard and Solberg were operating an identifiable hardware store. And Ole Amundsen's real estate business looked like the most profitable enterprise in the place. Signalling the new march of progress was Claresholm's formal incorporation as a village on June 15, four short weeks after Noble's arrival in the snow storm. Most citizens approved; those who were afraid of progress disapproved and opposed the idea of bringing a supply of domestic water from a neighboring farm by pipeline.

Noble found an available homestead quarter to suit him, less than three miles west of the village,[5] and then found an unoccupied cottage and rented it with a double purpose in mind. Naturally quick to sense opportunities, he knew he could use part of the cottage for a retail meat store which was needed in the village and the remaining part for living quarters for either one or two people.

Between wrapping parcels of beef and his duties on the new homestead, Charlie was too busy to be homesick or lonesome. Nevertheless, having obtained living accommodation that would serve two people as well as it would provide for one, why not send for Margaret? He wrote, proposing that she pack and come at once to meet him in Calgary, "Postal District of Alberta," to be married.

Margaret liked the idea and came promptly. Claresholm had a new Presbyterian minister, Peter Henderson, recently from Scotland and inducted into the little congregation at Claresholm just a couple of weeks earlier.[6] He was pleased to hear of the coming of another supporter of his denomination and further that Mr. Noble, who had been raised as an adherent of the Congregational Church, would henceforth be attending Presbyterian services.

The young minister with the thick Scottish brogue was delighted with the invitation to accompany Charlie Noble to

Calgary to perform the wedding ceremony. It was a bright and happy day, June 30, as Margaret and Charlie were married in the Queen's Hotel parlor in Calgary and then set out on their honeymoon consisting of the seventy-five mile train journey to Claresholm.

The Claresholm correspondent for the *Macleod Gazette* did not overlook the event and reported: "Mr. Noble, our meat merchant, returned on Saturday with his bride. We all join in offering our heartiest congratulations and wishing them a long and happy married life."[7]

As Margaret Noble might have expected, her husband, after little more than a month in residence, was already one of the busiest people, trying to be both a farmer and a businessman when either interest could demand a citizen's full time. Nor was the new Mrs. Noble to be much less busy as she responded to calls from outside her home. If a customer wanted a cut of meat when Charlie was absent on other duties, he or she would ring a bell and Margaret would come promptly to make the sale and wrap the goods. At the same time, she was working earnestly with Louise McKinney, the other Ontario-born girl who had just arrived by way of North Dakota and was bringing with her a great zeal for temperance organization and work, and also with Rev. Peter Henderson, who was hoping for the early construction of a church at Claresholm.

It seemed like a miracle, but within a few months the new church was built and dedicated and largely paid for with only eight charter members in the congregation, Mr. and Mrs. Noble and six others.[8]

How did it happen? It began when the ladies of Peter Henderson's little flock, still without their own church building, met at Mrs. Noble's home to form a Ladies' Aid.[9] It was obvious that the members were not going to be satisfied until they had their church, and before the onset of winter, they had it, a main structure twenty-four feet by thirty-six feet and a wing measuring eighteen feet by twenty feet. It was Claresholm's first church building, and with Scottish thrift and Presbyterian constancy, the total cost was $1,700.[10]

The reason for the low cost was simple enough: Ole Amundsen, who owned a big part of the village property, donated the site; William Moffat furnished lumber from his own lumberyard; and Charlie Miller and Charlie Noble — both experienced carpenters — did most of the work. The new church was dedicated and formally opened on December 11,

1904, and nobody had more reason for satisfaction than Mr. and Mrs. Charles Noble.[11]

Claresholm, which had been incorporated as a village in 1903, graduated to become an incorporated town two years later. At the first town election in September, 1905, William Moffat became the first mayor and Charles Noble became one of the first six councillors.[12] His election was further evidence of the rapid rate at which the Nobles had entered the life of the community. But the main impact of the Noble influence was yet to come.

4
BORN TO BE BUSY

Jemima Noble's second son was born to be busy and the Claresholm years confirmed it.

The thrifty and ambitious woman, for whom circumstances prevented no more than a slight retreat from poverty, would have enjoyed watching Charlie's energetic responses to the opportunities he saw everywhere on the new Canadian frontier. Torn between business prospects in the bustling young town of his choice and the ever present lure of farming on his own soil, he settled the internal dispute by plunging wholeheartedly into both. He remembered his mother's dictum: "Bite off more than you can chew, and chew it; plan more than you can do, and do it."

In the first three years at Claresholm, he was the local meat merchant, implement dealer, real estate agent, farmer, church builder, and town councillor, although not all at precisely the same time. Needless to say, he was busy, and Margaret — like many other brides before and since — wished he had more time to be at home, especially after their first son, Shirley Fraser, was born on July 1, 1906.

Charlie Noble's coming to the Northwest was primarily to obtain a homestead and farm, and it was logical that his first thoughts — except for the matter of marriage about that time — would be for the choice of an eligible quarter section with good soil moderately close to the railroad. If, as seemed likely, the place were to become the focal point of his social and business activities in the country, its location should be considered seriously.

A few homesteaders coming in the previous year had exercised their right to choose and had taken quarters close to the town site. Their assessments of scenery and distances were excellent, but as history showed convincingly, most of them were not good judges of soil. And as Charlie Noble discovered, there were still hundreds of choice places on the even-numbered sections from which to choose. After walking for a few days and studying soils, he fixed upon a situation three miles to the west and a jog north of the village. It was level and rich in its soil and offered a constant feast of Rocky Mountain scenery. Having satisfied himself about the goodness of the northwest quarter of Section 32 and convinced himself that Margaret would like it for a home site, he travelled down the line to the nearest dominion land office to pay a ten-dollar filing fee and make formal application.

Homestead regulations, revised slightly from time to time, made it clear that he, as head of a family or a male over the age of eighteen years, could file on any unassigned quarter on any even-numbered section — except sections 8 and 26 which were reserved for the Hudson's Bay Company — in Manitoba and the North West Territories. To qualify eventually for title, the homesteader would be required, in most cases, to erect a residence on the land, reside on same for at least six months in each of three years, and cultivate prescribed acreages. For a person in Noble's position, with a permanent dwelling so near, there was a new and helpful provision relaxing the residence requirement.

Charlie, prior to coming to Claresholm, entertained no thoughts about opening and operating a butcher shop. But the hamlet did not have such a facility, and it was a case of a job looking for a man who could handle it. He moved quickly, as was his custom, and when the local news correspondent reported the Noble marriage just five or six weeks after his arrival, the bridegroom was identified as "our meat merchant."[1]

When he rented a small house that would accommodate the proposed meat shop while serving as a home for himself and his bride, he was running the risk of displeasing Margaret. Some brides would have rebelled at a violation of their homes. The situation afforded a good test of a girl's resourcefulness and good nature, and the new Mrs. Noble passed with honors; not only did she accept the unesthetic association of home and meat store but also she willingly met customers and wrapped parcels of steaks and stewing meat when Charlie was busy elsewhere — which was most of the time.

To furnish stocks of meat for the trade, it was necessary for the retailer to buy quarters or halves of beef from nearby homesteaders for about 6 cents a pound or live steers or heifers at 3½ cents a pound and slaughter them on Section 32. But with no refrigeration, the merchant knew that fresh meats had to be sold on the day of delivery to his premises or they might never be sold, especially during spring and summer.

The meat business was never more than a sideline, but it provided a little additional revenue when the homestead was calling repeatedly for expenditures — barbed wire for fencing or lumber for an ox shelter or tools with which to dig a well. Allowing for bad debts and waste from spoiling, Mr. Noble estimated his profit from meat sales at one dollar a day. He wasn't complaining. Occasionally the "bad debts" turned out to be better than expected. Mr. Noble could tell of meeting a former Claresholm man on the main street in Lethbridge and hearing him admit that he had not forgotten a debt totalling forty dollars for meat bought thirty-five years earlier and wanted to make settlement then and there.

In service to the village, the meat store seemed to be important, and in January the news correspondent saw the owner building for the future, erecting an icehouse behind the butcher shop.[2] But after another four weeks, the owner was selling the meat business, intending to give more time to his new farm implement agency. The early 1904 news told of "Mr. Noble, our Massey Harris agent, building a large warehouse on Railway Street."[3] With rapid growth in the farming community and every farmer needing machinery, the implement trade was bound to be buoyant, at least as long as dealers were willing to accept lien notes payable "next November."

Massey Harris machines were popular, like Great Majestic kitchen ranges and J. I. Case steam engines. Disc harrows and cultivators bearing the "M H" trademark were selling faster than the factory could make deliveries. As for Massey Harris binders, dealers could advertise that they were the only ones on the market "with roller bearings throughout."

One of Noble's best lines was the new Verity sulky plow coming with wheels and the luxury of a seat for the operator. It took its name from the young Englishman who came to New York and then to Canada with some new and inventive ideas about making better farm equipment. Some of his best successes were with plows, stoves, sewing machines, and syrup kettles. The plows brought him his greatest fame, especially in the West, and for some years every farmer taking pride in his fields and furrows wanted a Verity plow. Noble, selling these new plows at fifty-three dollars each, placed forty-three of them in the 1904 season and took three more for work on his own expanding farms in that year of unusually heavy breaking activity.

When men talked about "breaking," they had to be thinking of either horses or prairie sod. When Noble was not cutting and weighing meat or selling plows during the first summer and fall, he was trying to make the tough prairie land ready for a 1904 crop. He managed to break fifty acres in the months of June and July — always the best months for plowing sod — using his primitive four-ox team for power. The furrows were the usual half mile in length although for the man between the plow handles, they seemed more like a mile and a half. To plow fifty acres, the oxen and driver would make a total of about 410 rounds or 410 miles with a twelve-inch walking plow. It would require a minimum of thirty full working days — not long enough for most drivers to cultivate an affection for their big and slow-moving ox critters.

Most homesteaders found a feeling of admiration for their horses but not for their oxen, and the big bovine brutes did not care. Noble was different from most homesteaders and remembered his oxen with a warm feeling. He even bragged about their size — an average weight of 1,800 pounds — and their willingness to walk along at a mile and a half an hour without motivation from a bullwhip. The four reds with moderately long horns and bored expressions were animals that Charlie Noble bought at beef prices when purchasing for his butcher shop. They may have served without enthusiasm, but they served well — as oxen served most owners well.

Noble was an experienced horseman when he filed on the Claresholm homestead, but he knew that until he was making his home on the farm and growing grain for feed, he would be better off with the kind of draft animals which could live off the land. That meant oxen. Horses, fashioned with a small stomach capacity, required feeds offering concentrated sources of energy, like oats or barley, along with hay to sustain them at work. Oxen, on the other hand, being endowed with huge rumens or first stomach compartments, could, if given time to fill up on grass or hay, find enough calories from such raw material to work for half a day. Thus there would not be a need of scarce and costly grain feeds. The homesteader without a stable and without a good selection of feeds was definitely better off with oxen than with horses, and Charlie Noble knew it.

Every ox, even though unloved, deserved a name, and Noble's oxen were suitably identified. The biggest and boniest, hinting that he might have been one of the seven lean and ill-favored kine from King Pharaoh's bad dreams, was called Goliath. Jonathon was the slowest and the one most in need of prodding if the work was to be completed. Ishmael was the most unpredictable ox when gadflies gave warning of egg-laying attack and the one which could and would drag the other members of the team to find refuge at the center of a nearby slough from the winged tormentors. And Joshua was the ox that never fully accepted the loss of his masculinity and liked to bellow in a deep voice that could be heard by impressionable cows grazing far beyond the homestead quarter.

The four oxen possessed individuality as well as muscle, but as Mr. Noble noted, they were equally adroit in lying low in morning grass and playing "lost" while their owner searched — sometimes for hours — to find them and bring them in for the day's work on the breaking plow.

Noble ran his furrows east and west on the homestead to insure the best possible view of the foothills and mountains for half of the time and the best view of the plains for the other half. His furrows were not always straight because the oxen had typical stubbornness and the plowman's thoughts were not always on plowing. But it did not matter greatly because the fields with crooked furrows seemed to be as productive and profitable as those with the best geometric lines.

Exactly what Noble was saying to the big oxen as the plow sliced off the twelve-inch ribbons of sod and turned them over is not known, but it seemed likely that the words were mild compared with what most draft oxen heard from their drivers. He was a mild-mannered man at any time and wise enough to know that cursing oxen achieved exactly nothing.

After breaking and discing the fifty acres in that first year and then acquiring more land, Noble recognized the need for a faster means of domesticating the wild sod land. Fifty acres a year would sound impressive in Iowa or Ontario, but it would not match the ambitious designs forming in his mind. A steam tractor appealed to him, but such a big purchase should be deferred for a while. The practical alternative was to supplement his own ox power with horses — perhaps hire fellow homesteaders with horse outfits to do custom breaking for him. Most homesteaders with the necessary power would welcome the chance to earn cash by working on another man's land. By one means or another, Noble saw five hundred acres of raw land being turned over and disced and made ready for seeding in the spring of 1905.

One who gladly accepted a contract to break on Noble's newly acquired land was Thomas Rutherford Cochrane, who came from North Dakota in 1904 and took a homestead about twenty miles east of Claresholm. Although raised in Iowa, Cochrane had lived near Knox, North Dakota, and knew Charlie Noble as a neighbor there. Cochrane and his son William brought horses and mules with them and were bringing two horses for Charlie Noble. The Cochranes, after locating their homesteads, drove to Claresholm, partly to renew acquaintances, partly to deliver the two horses that Noble wanted and needed. In the course of their visit, they heard that anybody in a position to undertake work with a breaking plow on Noble's land could qualify for payment of two dollars per acre.

The Cochranes were practical people, not long removed from Scotland, and knew that the time to make needed money was when work was available. They were in a position to field one walking plow with four horses and one plow with four mules and would be ready to start with a contract for twenty acres on a new farm southeast of Claresholm in a few days. "This," said William Cochrane many years later, "was probably the first land Mr. Noble had broken by contract in Alberta."[4]

What Charlie Noble saw of the two Cochrane plowing outfits confirmed his view that mules could outpull and outwork horses of equal size. A few years later he was keeping a high class jackass and was raising and using mules quite extensively.

One of the Cochrane mules, while plowing on the Noble land, won more attention than the others. He was the one known as Jack, and his great size and unusual sagacity were enough to bring him distinction. As William Cochrane recalled, the big mule's pulling power was the means of winning a few bets for his owner. When a nearby homesteader with a team of big but unsteady Clydesdales failed to dislodge a large stone firmly embedded in the ground ahead of the breaking plows, the elder Cochrane chided him to give up and give old Jack a chance to show what he could do. The neighbor scoffed and bet a dollar that the mule could not do it.

Jack was brought from the plow and hitched to the rock with a strong singletree. Cochrane, who had made certain that the mule had seen the slightly exposed rock, now spoke gently to the animal, telling him to ease slowly into the load and then give it all he had. Jack seemed to understand and responded exactly as instructed. The stone was seen to loosen just a little and then more and finally roll out upon the surface of the field. William Cochrane believed that Charlie Noble was present to enjoy the demonstration and see Tom Cochrane collect a dollar of bet money, saying that earning a dollar that way was much easier than having to plow half an acre for it.

For Mr. Noble, the Claresholm farming operations grew and prospered, just as anything he undertook would have to flourish or terminate. Farming which was at the ox team stage in 1903 and 1904 reached the Reeves steam tractor stage in 1908 and the Hart Parr gasoline tractor stage in 1909. The local newspaper reported in the latter year that: "Messrs. Milnes and Noble unloaded two fine big Hart Parr gasoline engines recently for use in their farming operations."[5]

The same issue of the *Claresholm Review* told of the same men having just bought the finest touring car ever seen in the district. "It is a handsome Reo and has all the latest wrinkles." The new car would serve two purposes, first in transporting land seekers and second in allowing Milnes and Noble to keep more closely in touch with their respective farms.

It was not their first car, as a news item from 1908 would show with a tinge of embarrassment not uncommon at that time: "D. M. Ross with a number of gentlemen started for Monarch Wednesday afternoon in Milne and Noble's auto. When about two and a half miles from town the hind axle broke and the party had to walk back to town."[6]

Noble's same changing farm operations could have been expressed by the figures for a mounting grain output. He harvested about 1,500 bushels of wheat from his first crop in 1904. Five years later, he was threshing 55,000 bushels of wheat and 14,400 bushels of oats.[7] Still this farming involvement did not restrict his other activities. He was selling more real estate than ever, selling Reeves steamers and Reo cars for which he and Milnes were agents,[8] serving on the town council, helping on the side of Mrs. Louise McKinney and other prohibitionists in the campaign preceding the Claresholm local option vote on November 24, 1908 — a losing effort in the light of the outcome — serving as a "pillar" in the Presbyterian church, conducting himself as an unfailing student of soils and agricultural practices, and helping as a member of the committee of directors to promote the Claresholm Agricultural Society.[9]

Charles Noble, it was said, was born to be busy, and the neighbors and friends in the frontier town marvelled at the long hours he kept and the magnitude of his accomplishments. They speculated that there were still bigger things ahead, and they were right.

5
MILNES AND NOBLE
REAL ESTATE
AND OTHER LINES

As the operation of a meat shop earning a dollar a day was a useful sideline helping to pay homestead expenses, so Charlie Noble's real estate business in association with T. C. Milnes was an extremely big sideline with earnings being used to finance new farming ventures. Moreover, those hectic days in land sales constituted an important chapter in his life and in the life of the community.

It was on a bright June morning that Mr. Milnes, a newcomer from Indiana, drove his buggy team of well fed and spirited roadsters from Claresholm to the Noble homestead to present Charlie with a proposal that they join as partners to buy and sell real estate. Noble was still breaking the prairie sod, hoping to enlarge the area of homestead cultivation. When Milnes overtook him about midway across the field, there he was between the handles of his plow, walking in the furrow in bare feet and looking quite contented with the task of trying to keep three oxen and one horse travelling in a proper manner and in the proper direction.

The reason for the bare feet was not discussed, but various explanations were proposed later, among them that the homesteader did not have a pair of boots at that time or was simply sparing the pair he had. It was another opinion that he was in bare feet because he liked the feel of the cool and moist soil between his toes. To those who understood the nature of the man, the conservation theory was the more plausible. But regardless of other factors, bare feet could have been preferable to sweaty feet impounded in stiff and ill-fitting leather boots, and they would certainly serve to create a surer feeling of kinship between the man and his earth.

Whatever else may be said, that soil was gripping Charlie Noble as he had never been gripped before. He wondered as he plowed if the Indians of certain tribes were right in their belief about the Great Spirit choosing to live in the soil rather than in the skies. Anyway, for the next fifty years, Noble's feet were to remain close to the soil, and so was his heart.

As Milnes found Noble on that June day, the homesteader was renewing his determination that regardless of other activities, his primary objective was to farm and set a high standard in farming. He had sold his meat business to a fellow townsman, Curnock by name, and his implement agency to another Claresholm man, Mr. Wannamaker, but was not ruling out the possibility of new enterprises that would support or advance his farming goal.

Milnes was a businessman more than a farmer as his freshly painted buggy and well groomed appearance showed clearly. He came to the Canadian West quite casually, with no preconceived ideas about staying. But circumstances can play strange tricks on people. Milnes had arrived in March, 1905, and the introduction to the country was not conducive to staying. His visit coincided with a March blizzard carrying heavy snow and winter fury on a northwest wind. The outlook was bleak, and Milnes, who found himself stranded at Claresholm with totally inadequate clothing, enquired about the next train that would take him back in the general direction of Indiana and home. The reply was not encouraging: "No train out for two days."

In the meantime, the storm ended, and the sun shone gloriously making everybody, including Milnes, forget about the winter blast. Instead of taking the next train south, he bought a section of land near Claresholm, then rented a space in the village to serve as an office and sent a message to his wife and family directing them to join him as soon as the school term ended in June.

Milnes was a tall, rather dignified man, very successful in every business venture he had ever undertaken, and as time was to show, the same sort of success would follow him into Alberta. In addition to being successful at real estate and farming, he became mayor of Claresholm in 1911 and was elected to the Alberta Legislature in 1921, defeating Louise

McKinney, who had been sitting as the first lady member of a legislature in Canada.

"Where's the other ox?" the well dressed Milnes asked as he sat in his buggy on that warm June morning, attempting to assess this odd combination comprising three big oxen, one small horse, and a dishevelled plowman.

"I told him the other ox was indisposed," Noble reported later. Then after a few seconds of hesitation, the real answer was given: "I bought the four oxen for $300, on time, and worked them hard all spring. The big dark one got thin so I laid him off for a while to cheer him up because I think I can sell the four of them to Dr. Tupper for enough cash to pay the note. That way, I will have had the use of them at no cash cost."

Milnes was impressed, and throwing the leather reins over the dashboard, he dismounted from the buggy and came directly to the point of his visit. As Noble told it later, Milnes said he was looking for "a frank kind of man who could look after himself in a deal to join him in business."

Noble was not ready for the surprise of an implied proposition like this, and while he was searching for a reply, Milnes offered further comment that was not forgotten: "But you'd need to wash up and get some shoes and nice clothes."[1]

Charlie Noble was not worried about the necessity of wearing shoes and presenting a clean face because he was normally clean and tidy in his habits, but he wanted to know more about Milnes's manner of conducting business. Aware of his own fondness for freedom, he enquired if Milnes thought he could be a useful partner without being tied down or restricted to one job.

Milnes laughed and gave assurance that he did not want a partner who would be satisfied to stay at one job. In his own way of life, Milnes said, he demanded variety, and he would be surprised if a Milnes and Noble partnership would ever be restricted to real estate.

Noble agreed to become a partner in the proposed enterprise, with the understanding that he would not be expected to change his plans for farming in a bigger way. Milnes agreed and added that they might both be farming on a bigger scale.

Milnes had the benefit of more business experience and was a skillful organizer and office administrator, while Noble was at his best in the outdoors. Together, they would make an excellent team and were soon setting high standards in business. Both had friends in the United States, Milnes in the East and Noble in the Midwest, enough to give Milnes and

Noble a distinct advantage at a time when the tide of immigration was rising and Americans were sensing their own limitations in land. Some 3,000 American settlers came by way of Lethbridge during the year ending at June 30, 1903, of whom 2,144 located in the district of Alberta. Claresholm seemed to be the name that was best known to the newcomers from the south.

Most of those coming from the United States were looking for homesteads, but many others were bringing capital and showing interest in buying either improved or unimproved farms of size. Some American buyers did not appear at all but in their eagerness to become owners of new and low-priced land in the Canadian West, sent sums of money to Noble or Milnes with instructions to buy a quarter or half or section of land such as "you'd like to buy for yourself."

Largely due to Milnes and Noble and their popularity with American buyers, real estate became Claresholm's leading business, bearing a resemblance to the Calgary boom of 1911 and 1912 when the city license inspector could report 443 licensed real estate agencies and believed the total sales force would number at least 2,000 individuals.

The Claresholm situation attracted many others who aspired to sell real estate, and competition became keen and business ethics may have deteriorated. It was a Milnes and Noble policy from the outset to insure that visitors showing an interest in purchasing land would receive every attention short of being supplied with liquor. The partners maintained rubber-tired buggies and beautiful horses by which to transport clients to inspect properties, and then, in 1907, they added a motor car while such a vehicle was still a novelty at Claresholm. There was nothing wrong with that, but the editor in the nearby town of Nanton believed some Claresholm salesmen were going too far in entertainment and offering to "throw in the climate."

Charlie Noble recalled the listing of a certain quarter section known to be hopelessly littered with field stones. Most candidates for purchase were sufficiently familiar with stones and the hated task of picking them without ever getting the last one to rudely shun the land in question — about the way they would avoid an exposure to smallpox. But a not-too-scrupulous salesman made a bet that he could sell the quarter. Finding a remittance man with more money than judgment, the salesman congratulated him on his interest in buying a piece of land and invited him to inspect a quarter section he was in a position to sell. As the well groomed and soft-spoken young fellow from

England was being conveyed by horse and buggy to the property, the salesman took care to mention the stones before the prospective customer saw them.

"You'll see some rocks on this place," he said, "but you must understand that they do not go with the farm. The present owner is willing to sell the land, but he wants to reserve the stones for sale to contractors during the building boom he sees coming in this community."

The naive customer reacted in anger, saying: "The bloody nerve of the owner! He can't get away with that. If I buy the farm, I want all the resources. I'll buy the farm as it is or I will not buy it at all."

It was the pronouncement for which the salesman had hoped and he replied condescendingly that if the buyer felt that way, he could make a written offer to purchase the farm with "all the building stones included" and see how the seller would react. The firm offer was made, and needless to say, the owner of the problem quarter section was happy to accept.

The demand for the building stones did not materialize, but Claresholm was booming and its pioneer real estate agents, namely Milnes and Noble, were largely responsible for the public interest that started it. A writer for the *Manitoba Free Press* made a special visit to the district in 1907 and was not disappointed. After meeting with Ole Amundsen, T. C. Milnes, Charles Noble, and Nick Taitenger, who settled eleven miles east of Claresholm in 1903 and four years later won the world championship for barley at the international show in Chicago, the reporter became "fired up" in his enthusiasm about what he termed this "Dizzy Little Town" and its surrounding farm land. The Claresholm citizens read it with a mixture of amusement and pride, and the editor of the *Claresholm Review* was pleased to copy it:

> I have seen towns and towns! But for up-to-date methods of doing business, wide-awake alertness and genuine "get-a-move-on Sonny" air, commend me to the swagger little town of Claresholm, set in fastness of the Crow's Nest line.
>
> Claresholm is just four years old but it has all its teeth — including wisdom teeth — and is able to toddle alone. There isn't an inch of ground belonging to speculators — not an acre of earth that isn't busy. Not alone a summer wheat country is this district, but a winter wheat world as well. When I visited Claresholm,

Sept. 19, 20, 21, the binders were hugging the sheaves of
1907 growth, and across the way six inches of [winter]
wheat looked up promisingly green. The plow was at
work — not the single furrow plow of "gee-haw"
memory, but a giant wheeled thing of 110 horse power,
turning up 45 acres of ground a day, in furrows as
straight as a school pencil.

Dizzy little town? Well, rather. Land $4.00 an acre in
1904 selling in 1907 at $50 an acre. Four years ago a flag
station; today 1,000 souls and every homestead for 50
miles out taken. Amundsen, the first settler, will market
30,000 bushels of grain off 500 acres. Milnes, a neighbor,
has 1,200 acres in grain. Noble's farm of 2,500 acres
yielded almost 13,000 bushels in 1906 and another
American hustler named McLean, has 1,000 acres ready
for 1908, just because 500 acres in 1907 put him in good
cash humor.

Claresholm has a smart newspaper chock full of paid
ads; the shops are general in kind and the rival banks do
a big business. The manager of the big bank is president
of the Board of Trade. . . . Real estate men chase the
western states for monied men, invite them to Claresholm and give them the time of their lives when they
come. They also give them the chance to buy land at $45
and $50 an acre.

All around you see green fields and grazing runs.
Everywhere you see prosperity and public spirit. And
the people? The "whitest" on earth — welcoming the
stranger and speeding the parting guest.[2]

It was a wonder that the reporter got out of the "Dizzy Little
Town" without being persuaded to buy a parcel of real estate.
Many others who came without thought of purchasing were
more or less mesmerized into purchases and left as land owners,
including some of Charlie Noble's relatives. The local paper
mentioned one of these: "Mr. [Henry] Sherwood, who comes
from Illinois, was here this week visiting his nephew, Mr. C. S.
Noble. He left on Monday to visit Banff. While here, Mr.
Sherwood followed the example of all bright Americans and
bought a piece of Claresholm real estate.[3]

Land prices were rising rapidly. It was announced in March,
1906, that all CPR land would, henceforth, carry a minimum
price of six dollars per acre. But interest and demand did not
slacken, and the Milnes and Noble touring car remained almost

constantly on the road, taking prospective buyers back and forth. The heavy crop in 1908 — thirty-five bushels of wheat per acre on Noble's land — was further incentive, and a growing number of Americans who heard about Milnes and Noble were buying rail tickets to Claresholm.

Readers of the *Claresholm Review* were informed about Milnes and Noble sales quite often, but only the big sales seemed to warrant space. They would read, for example, that: "Messrs. Milnes and Noble this week put through a big real estate deal, selling 1,600 acres northeast of Claresholm to Mr. Ole Arnegard, a well known North Dakota banker,"[4] or days later that: "One man who bought 960 acres this week will break it all this year."[5]

Although Milnes and Noble's business card said "Real Estate, Loans, and Insurance," the fact was that the partners possessed some of the characteristics of the old-time district handyman who could witch wells, pour babbitt, emasculate colts, and respond to almost any call. The partners did not perform barnyard chores, but in business matters their services were sometimes beyond description. The local press told of their undertaking to sell and distribute the tractor monsters of their time, the Reeves steamers, and then in early 1909 taking the agency for the Reo auto and "unloading five cars this week, two big cars and three roadsters. The firm finds the Reo a popular car in Southern Alberta."[6]

Perhaps it was incorrect to write that Milnes and Noble did not perform barnyard tasks because the weekly newspaper, which unwittingly managed to capture much of local history, reported the shipment by the partners of a carload "of hogs to Lethbridge on Monday last. This is, we believe, the first carload shipped out of Claresholm."[7]

Clarlie Noble always admired versatility displayed by a good mixed farmer, and when asked about the amazingly diversified nature of his business services, he answered that he and his partner were striving to bring the mixed farming principle into the town's business offices.

One way or another, Milnes and Noble served their community well, but late in 1908 when the election of members to the town council was being called, Charlie Noble was not a candidate. In declining a nomination, he was giving a hint of another move in the fulfillment of a dream. He would be terminating his residence in Claresholm but not his business association with his partner and friend, T. C. Milnes.

6
TO A PLACE
CALLED NOBLE

They were thirty-four bumpy and hazardous trail miles by
Reo auto from Claresholm to the new residence at a place
called Noble, and on a mid-August day in 1909, Charlie and
Margaret Noble, infant sons Shirley and Gerald, and the caged
family canary were moving. The *Claresholm Review* treated
the event briefly, noting that: "Mr. C. S. Noble moved his
household effects to the new town of Noble this week and will
take up residence in his new house built there this summer."[1]
It was still regarded as a triumph to travel that far on Alberta
roads by automobile without a breakdown or a long delay in
one of the numerous country mudholes. Charlie Noble, however, had taken prospective land buyers in that direction on
various occasions and knew how to escape the worst of the
mud-and-water obstacles.
As the man in the driver's seat, Noble had no worries about
other motor traffic. On an average day he could expect to make
that long trip without as much as seeing another mechanical
vehicle, and if he did encounter one, the novelty and fraternal
feeling would compel both drivers to stop long enough to
exchange greetings and information about trails. The biggest
threat to public safety was the one felt by drivers of
horse-drawn buggies and wagons whose fear-filled animals
wanted to turn around in their harness and stage a runaway.
The wise horseman, seeing or hearing the approach of the Reo
or any other similar mechanical monster, lost no time in driving
his horses as far as possible off the trail and maintaining the
distance until the source of hysteria had passed.

The Nobles were prepared for the journey, as much prepared as they could be. They carried a can of gasoline, an auxiliary supply of calcium carbide for the lamps, and a tire repair kit that could be put to use at any point on the trail. The babies were well wrapped to shield them from those extra breezes generated at speeds of fifteen and twenty miles per hour. Charlie, as the driver, wore goggles and an automobilist's leather cap, and Margaret, riding in the back seat with the children, wore a veil drawn tightly over her hat and hair and a long duster garment designed especially for lady passengers in open cars. When the two infant sons went to sleep, she was free to hold the cage containing her precious canary outside the car where there would be less exposure to motor fumes readily detected on the inside.

Mr. and Mrs. Noble were sorry to be leaving their three-storey house — one of the biggest and finest in Claresholm — and the association of many friends made there. That big square house with handsome veranda, their second home in Claresholm, was being taken over by T. C. Milnes and would someday become the Claresholm hospital.

The people on the street told them how much they would be missed, and the Nobles realized how deeply their social as well as business roots had penetrated the neighborhood soil in six years. They would miss the friends with whom they had shared struggles in founding the community, men like the tireless Ole Amundsen, who was the first to catch a vision of a flourishing town, and William Moffat, who arrived with several carloads of lumber for the initial buildings and having stacked the wood on the prairie, sat on the highest pile and waited for buyers.[2] Certainly, they would miss the six-year friendship of Rev. Peter Henderson for whom the marriage ceremony uniting Charles and Margaret Noble was the first after his coming from Scotland. Henderson left Claresholm to accept a bigger church charge at Montreal but was then glad to accept an invitation to return to the Alberta town. Four years after signing the marriage certificate of Charles and Margaret Noble, he was officiating at the wedding of Annie Fraser — Mrs. Noble's sister — and William Buchanan, an implement dealer at nearby Granum. Miss Annie had come from Ontario to visit two sisters and a brother then living at Claresholm, and in the frontier land dominated by unwilling bachelors, she soon found reason to remain and the wedding was at the Noble home.[3] The other Fraser girl was Alexandrina, who had come to serve as office secretary for Milnes and Noble, and the brother was the Rev.

Simon L. Fraser, who made Charlie Noble's acquaintance at Knox, North Dakota, then came to a Presbyterian church assignment at Stavely, and finally left the church to divide his time between farming nearby and real estate in Claresholm. For Mrs. Noble, departure from Claresholm was now very much like "leaving home."

In mid-September, after becoming settled in the new house beside the new railway line being built from Kipp in the general direction of Calgary, the Nobles were back at Claresholm for a visit and a round of neighborly parties conducted with small-town warmth unknown in bigger places.[4]

In making the move eastward from Claresholm, Charlie Noble was not terminating the most successful partnership of Milnes and Noble. The focal point of land sales had been shifting in that direction, and Charlie was not long at the new location before opening another real estate office. Having bought and sold much of the land around Claresholm and having seen it settled, there was no longer much chance of assembling big parcels of the kind in which he had been specializing. He may have felt the local competition in real estate created by his brother-in-law, Simon Fraser, but Charlie was becoming more like a real estate consultant with a thorough knowledge of land over a broad area. Moreover, Charlie had always known a fondness for new adventure. He knew from experience that there comes a time when a fresh frontier is nigh irresistible again.

The new life was for him, and the more he saw of the rich brown loam of the area about midway between Claresholm and Lethbridge, the better he liked it. He recalled his first land sales near the new railroad point of Noble. He had a block consisting of nine quarters on his sales list and told Milnes of his hope of finding a buyer. Milnes laughed and said the land was too far back for people intending to farm. But impressed by the high quality of the soil, Noble was fired with determination and visited his banker to drop the idea of this property being a good investment for one or more of the bank's clients. The banker agreed and invited nine of the town's businessmen to meet Noble at the bank office. Before the end of the meeting, the nine quarters were sold to eight of the nine clients and the bank manager.

Charlie was selling more and more of the CPR land in the new district, largely to American buyers who were relying on his advice. Dave Ugland of Devil's Lake, an acquaintance, was sending many interested North Dakotans directly to Noble, assuring them that with CPR land to choose from and Noble to advise them, they would find exactly what they wanted. The pioneer railroad company, as reported about that time, had qualified for land grants totalling 26,710,000 acres and sold, up to June 30, 1907, about 18,000,000 acres. Prices were rising and had averaged about eight dollars per acre in that recent year. There was still much railroad land to sell, and the new prices ranging between ten and fifteen dollars an acre were not deterring sales.

Naturally, interest in CPR land was quickened when it was announced in 1908 that a branch line would be built from Kipp to Aldersyde to give Calgary and Lethbridge a more direct connection. And now, whether by good judgment or good fortune on Noble's part, the rails would traverse his favorite area. Then, to bring him more closely into the weave of area development, he was authorized by the railroad company to buy needed town site land along the route. By making their purchases in this manner, company officials hoped to escape the costliness of land rush prices.

Here, Noble could consolidate his farming enterprise in one or two big units, something he could no longer do at Claresholm, where his land holdings were scattered. In the new district he could still emulate the area's first settler, J. W. McClain from California, who bought CPR land in 1904 and broke 450 acres in the "far out" district in his first year and was rewarded with a big crop in 1905.

Noble's real estate business had been profitable, and with money in the bank, he bought 4½ sections about four miles west of where Nobleford was to be built, even before the new railroad was announced. This land, upon development, became Mountain View Farm. And in 1909 he made the still bigger purchase of the land on which the famous Grand View Farm was formed.

The latter purchase happened this way: As a real estate agent, he invited a possible purchaser to inspect these sections beside the projected railway and found the person being overly cautious. "This," said Noble, "is an opportunity you should not reject, and if you don't buy the land, I will buy it for myself."

The interested party could not bring himself to buy so much land, whereupon Noble promptly redeemed himself, paid a few thousand dollars in cash, and assumed an obligation to meet a new debt of $80,000 on this spread of 5,520 acres, part of it to the CPR, most of it to the McCormick Estates of Pendleton, Oregon. The price was twenty-five dollars per acre.

With railroad construction proceeding from the Kipp end of the line, the Monarch town site was the first to catch attention and the first from which building lots were offered. O. M. Ross was the local mogul making sales in the summer of 1908, and the manner of promotion gave the impression that Monarch would become a metropolis likely to rival Lethbridge or Calgary. One of those listed among the buyers of lots was W. H. Fairfield, who came to the area as an irrigation specialist in 1901 and was later appointed to the position of superintendent of the new and treeless experimental station at Lethbridge.[5] Dr. Fairfield, whose name had a familiar ring across the West in later years, paid seventy-five dollars for his Monarch lot, no doubt with the idea of building a home there.

Late in 1909, the railroad was completed as far north as the Little Bow River where the Carmangay town site was laid out, and the village lots were placed on the market. C. W. Carman and his wife, Gay, who came from Chicago, bringing substantial capital, gave their names to the new place and became the first big farm operators in the district. Then, when lots were offered and $50,000 worth of the new town site property was sold by auction on July 20, 1909, Mr. Carman was the biggest single purchaser, paying from fifty to one hundred dollars each for his lots.[6]

The new town site of Noble was next, and people in the area read that the CPR had bought "a town site and named it after the popular Claresholm man." The rest of the story as it appeared in May, 1909, told that: "The town of Noble is the latest. Mr. Noble has sold the land in [section] 11-13-23-W of 4 on the Carmangay-Lethbridge line [to the CPR] and it will be surveyed at once as a townsite and will be on the market shortly. The C.P.R. [has] honored Mr. Noble by naming the town after him and it is understood he will build a fine home in the new town. He has sold his Claresholm house to his partner, Mr. Milnes. The town of Noble to be, is well situated to become an important point. It is expected that an elevator will be built this summer and the C.P.R. will haul grain from there this fall."[7]

The new town site was surveyed with all the dispatch which would have been expected if Charlie Noble had been doing it. Without delay, the lots were offered for sale. Just as C. W. Carman was the principal buyer of lots at the village bearing his name, so Charles Noble was the leading buyer of the Noble subdivision property. It seemed strange that he was buying lots of the land he had so recently sold to the railroad company, but it was the orderly way to proceed. There was another difference between the purchases made by Mr. Carman and Mr. Noble: The latter was paying higher prices for the lots of his choosing, generally $100 per lot, but for one lot considered better than others, he paid $600.

The CPR records showed thirteen lots being bought by Mr. Noble and three more by Milnes and Noble.[8]

The hunger for western land in parcels of any size was like the hunger for bread, a writer for the *Lethbridge Daily Herald* noted with satisfaction. During the single month of September, the Dominion Land Office at Lethbridge processed 438 formal entries for homesteads in the area and 301 entries for pre-emptions, thus accounting for 739 quarter sections. The biggest single day in the month was Monday, September 20, when eight new townships in Alberta's dry southeast — south of Whitla and Seven Persons — were thrown open for homesteading. It brought a land rush such as Lethbridge people had not previously witnessed. The most eager ones arrived at the entrance to the land office five days before the filing date, and with each passing day, the crowd became a little bigger until the officials found it necessary to construct a chute patterned after stockyard facilities in order to exercise control. When the gate was opened on the morning of the first day for filing, Paul Meister from Columbus, Ohio, was the first to squeeze in, and the several hundred spectators who had assembled to watch the rush cheered their approval for the display of human endurance, all for a quarter section in an area which was of doubtful value for farming.[9]

The construction of Mr. Noble's high house on farm land east of the railroad tracks was the first to receive his attention. Stabling for horses and mules followed, and for the next year he was building on a grand scale in the hamlet and on the nearby farms. Others, by this time, were building too. A railway station was erected and Mat McGregor constructed and opened a store building. The Norris Grain Company built an elevator beside the track to furnish the typical village break in the prairie skyline. And while this was going on, Mr. Noble was embarking upon the construction of his office to accommodate the Milnes and Noble business.

Although started without formality, that office structure's beginning seemed to coincide exactly with the laying of the cornerstone of Alberta's handsome Legislative Building in Edmonton on the first day of October, with Governor General Earl Grey performing the honors. Three days later, His

Excellency was engaged in precisely the same duties in connection with Saskatchewan's Legislative Building at Regina.

Noble and his friends might look upon his new building as an office, but it was much more; it was there that the first church services were conducted in the village and there, also, that the first school classes were conducted almost a year before Nobleford had a real school.

The first grain was shipped from Noble at the end of November, sixteen carloads of it and all from Mr. Noble's Mountain View Farm, which had come under the influence of the breaking plow and into production a year earlier than the Grand View place beside the hamlet.[10] The thirty-two-horsepower Reeves cross compound steam tractor bought to serve the Noble farms near Claresholm was transferred to what would become the Mountain View place for breaking in 1908 and then to the Grand View land in the next year.

In using this big steamer — representative of a race of monsters said to be effective in breaking their owners as well as the prairie sod — Noble worked out a first-plowing technique for native grassland which won widespread attention. It began with shallow plowing and a 1000-pound, cement-filled roller pulled behind the plows, obviously a job for a steam engine or an equally powerful gasoline tractor. The heavy roller would effectively flatten the sod furrows, giving the native root masses the best chance to rot quickly and leaving the furrowed surface in an ideal state for discing. The roller, according to Mr. Noble, left the fields so level and smooth that he could drive his Reo automobile across them at twenty miles an hour, a greater speed than most motorists would choose for driving on Alberta roads at that time.

Too often in farm practice, the fresh sod furrows from the breaking plows were poorly turned and allowed to lose their moisture before being pressed against the subsoil and worked into a state of cultivation by means of discs. Anyone who, like Noble or H. W. Campbell, had studied summerfallowing methods knew that moisture that escapes by evaporation will not be recovered and part of the reason for summerfallowing will be defeated.

A poor job of breaking that permitted the topsoil to furrow depth to become completely dried out held the single advantage of insuring a quicker killing of native grasses, but at the high price of lost moisture likely to result in reduced yields in the first crop year. Noble's method explained why his crops in the first year after breaking were consistently higher in yields than those of neighbors who followed more common practices. The yield differences were demonstrated clearly in 1910.

This technique of rolling the land immediately after the breaking plows, thoroughly discing during the summer, and backsetting in the autumn came up for unscheduled discussions at the prestigious Dry Farming Congress held at Billings, Montana, in 1909, at which Charlie Noble was in attendance. Among the Canadians present as official representatives and as self-assigned guardians of the soil were some of the country's leading figures in agriculture. As a consequence, Charles Noble was, for the first time, mingling with agricultural scientists and leaders like W. H. Fairfield, who was superintendent of the dominion experimental station at Lethbridge; John Bracken, who was soon to become professor of field husbandry at the University of Saskatchewan and still later, premier of Manitoba; George Harcourt, deputy minister of agriculture in Alberta; and Hon. W. R. Motherwell, who was attending as minister of agriculture in Saskatchewan and was to become, a few years later, one of Canada's most highly respected federal ministers of agriculture. Noble was also able to renew his acquaintance of two years with H. W. "Dustmulch Campbell," who was still captivating western audiences with his message about dry land farming. A reporter described Campbell as the most popular of the Congress speakers, and Noble and Campbell greeted each other like old friends.[11]

As Campbell two years earlier had reinforced Noble's dedication to soil care and soil studies, the Dry Farming Congress program of 1909 inspired a new determination to match the large size of his farming operations with the most progressive methods and practices available to him.

It was good for an enterprising man of the soil such as Charles Noble to be meeting and mingling with men of prominence and influence such as he met at Billings. It was good, also, for them to be meeting and mingling with him.

7
THE SPIRIT OF
DRY FARMING, 1912

Charlie Noble's first crop year in the new prairie location where the village bearing his name was taking shape was downright disappointing, almost ruinous. The total precipitation of 7.9 inches recorded at nearby Lethbridge made 1910 the driest year in the memory of local people. And not until 1926, when the precipitation figure fell to 7.63 inches, did southern Albertans see its drought equivalent again. Even the best of land preparation as carried out by Noble's methods could not offset the depressing effect of a paltry 1 inch of rainfall in June and 1.5 inches in July.

It would have been easy for the big farmer to see his recent move toward the heart of the prairie country as a mistake, had it not been known that most other parts — including Claresholm — were in the grip of drought at the same time. At Calgary, where precipitation of 17.43 inches was regarded as normal, the year's total was only 12.03 inches, and at Prince Albert, where the normal was 15.5 inches, only 8 inches was recorded.

Many crops in that year were a complete failure, even on first-crop land where the new breaking had been allowed to become dried out before being pressed down and disced. Wheat on Noble's well prepared breaking was not a total failure, but the returns came far short of meeting capital debt obligations and operating expenses. The Pendleton people in Oregon, from whom he had bought the Grand View property, would have to wait for their money.

But a dry year, like other forms of setback, carried lessons for all settlers, among them that western growers are constantly at the mercy of the weather and that any previously experienced weather extremes can come again and probably will. Farmers and others, while hoping for the best, should be preparing for the worst.

That same year of drought had another effect: If it had done nothing more of value, it had certainly intensified prairie interest in the young and vigorous International Dry Farming Congress and its purposes. Charlie Noble attended the Congress meetings at Billings, Montana, in 1909 and returned home with rejuvenated enthusiasm for the broad tasks of land care and conservation in areas where Mother Nature was stingy in dispensing moisture.

The Dry Farming Congress, which held its first conference at Denver in 1907, had gained spectacularly in prominence and prestige. Born in the minds of midwestern Americans realizing that semiarid soils — with annual precipitation of less than twenty inches — required special attention and special methods in culture, the Congress had become a big child in a remarkably short time. The fact that more than one quarter of the arable land on the North American continent was in this category should have removed all doubt about the importance of the purposes of such an organization. By 1910, the supporters of the Congress — of whom Charlie Noble was one of the most enthusiastic — could boast that it was the biggest and most vocal agricultural organization of its kind in the world. By 1911, it had 13,500 individual members in fifty countries.[1] Suddenly, it had become an agricultural and a political giant, and prime ministers, presidents, and secretaries of agriculture were taking notice and listening.

The conference of 1910 was at Spokane and the one of 1911 at Colorado Springs, where it shared public attention with the International Congress of Farm Women, meeting for the first time. Alberta's agricultural leaders and members of the Lethbridge Board of Trade did not hide their desire to see the big Congress meetings and contests of 1912 held at Lethbridge, where interest was obvious. Over one hundred Albertans travelling by special train from Lethbridge — seventy-five dollars for return fare with sleeping berths included — descended upon Colorado Springs in October, 1911, taking with them many high class exhibits, a Scottish pipe band, and the country's best orators, like Hon. Duncan Marshall from the Alberta government and Hon. W. R. Motherwell from Saskatchewan. Neither Marshall nor Motherwell was showing any exhaustion from the supporting roles they had been playing in the federal general election held a few days earlier, September 21, when Sir Wilfrid Laurier's proposed reciprocity deal with the United States was defeated, mainly because of the eastern opposition.

The Alberta display of agricultural products, when set up in competitive form, won the trophy for the best state or provincial exhibit from anywhere in the world. One way or another, the Canadians seemed to dominate the Congress program at Colorado Springs to such an extent that Salt Lake City and Prescott, Arizona, considered the leading contenders for the right to hold the 1912 Congress meetings, withdrew, and Lethbridge was named to be the next conference city.

There was loud jubilation in the Canadian ranks, and the Alberta delegates returned home to a heroes' welcome that would have pleased even a winning Grey Cup football team of later years. There were repeated pledges to make the 1912 Congress assembly the best ever and to use it to demonstrate more clearly than ever before the goodness of western Canadian soil. It would be a joint effort, bringing town and country together. The board of trade could be expected to be motivated by business ambitions, but there were enough farming people like Charles Noble to insure that the place of agricultural education and conservation would be first and foremost.

Noble was not one of the orators. He would always feel more at ease with a scoop shovel or a brace of leather lines to a team of mules than with a place on a public platform, but at Congress sessions, no human figure stood out more conspicuously than that of this tall, straight, muscular, and rather bashful man wearing a well pressed suit. He was listening to everything, making notes, and saying very little. At sessions touching upon his special interests — meaning soil management, conservation, field power, and crops — he was likely to be sitting in the front row where there would be a minimum of distractions. That was where he sat for lectures by his friend H. W. Campbell and there also for the Congress paper on flax presented by Prof. H. L. Bolley from the North Dakota Agricultural College. Flax, said the professor, took less moisture from the soil than other common crops like wheat, oats, and barley and deserved a more prominent place in dry land crop planning than it had received. Noble, who was constantly in search of new and better crops and better methods and had been thinking seriously about flax as a crop for southern Alberta, was now convinced. As a man of action, he began at once to enquire about the best varieties and sources of seed.

The local committee appointed at Lethbridge and the *Lethbridge Daily Herald* did not let Alberta people forget about the international farm festival which would be held between October 19 and 26, 1912. Preparation for exhibits, contests, judges, accommodation for meetings, and living accommodation for visitors seemed endless. Lethbridge as well as Alberta agriculture was on test, and citizens were entering into the spirit of an international congress and showing determination to make it at least as much of a success as the first Calgary Stampede to be held just about a month earlier.

The prizes offered in the many competitions were of a kind and value never before assembled as agricultural awards. The prize for the best bushel of hard wheat — open to the world and bound to be the biggest class in the show — was no less than a Rumely Oil-Pull tractor valued at $2500 and donated by the Rumely Company of La Porte, Indiana. This grand prize would be delivered by the donor to the winner at any point in Canada or the United States.

The best sheaf of hard wheat, also open to the world, would qualify for a Stewart sheaf loader valued at $500, while the best sheaf of oats would get a McCormick binder, and the best sheaf of barley, a John Deere binder. What prizes! As would be expected, the entries were numerous.

There were some disappointments, of course. President Taft of the United States was unable to keep his appointment at Lethbridge, and Canada's Prime Minister Borden was likewise obliged to communicate his regrets. But Lethbridge had no reason to be disappointed with the general response. Exhibits and visitors poured in for the sixth International Dry Farming Congress. Russia, Holland, Palestine, China, Persia, England, Germany, and Australia, as well as most parts of Canada and the United States, were represented, bringing reassurance to John T. Burns, the general secretary of the Congress and the man whose confidence about the need for a congress had sustained the movement from its beginning. He was repeating the sentiment he had sounded before, the need to "conquer drought through scientific soil management and moisture conservation." It would bring "agricultural uplift throughout the world.[2]

With displays of the world's best in agricultural products and lectures on a multiplicity of agricultural subjects, Charlie Noble said it was like a postgraduate course on farming. The principle of mixed farming was eloquently proclaimed again. Some of the first clear warnings about the dangers of dust mulch summer-fallowing as a contributor to soil drifting were sounded. Tree planting to protect fields and farmsteads was recommended again, without opposition. The liveliest controversy in the lecture halls was kindled by the speaker dealing with tractor power when he declared that horses for field work would soon be a thing of the past. He should have known better than to hurl offense at the loyal horsemen, still outnumbering the backers of tractor power by ten to one.

Not far away, however, was the most modern display of tractors and machines that had been seen anywhere short of the Winnipeg Motor Competitions, pointing moderately clearly to the future. Charlie Noble, wishing to be at several places at once, was giving as much of his time as possible to the tractors, trying to see both the steam and gasoline giants in an impartial light. He was not deserting the friendly horses and mules with which he had had lifelong contact, but he was interested in the most economical power for his operations and was not overlooking a hope that the day would come when all domestic animals would be spared the cruel toil of field work, especially when driven by merciless humans.

As the Congress displays demonstrated, the big steam tractors were still being promoted by confident manufacturers and salesmen, but the noisy gasoline-powered machines were getting more attention and outnumbered the steamers on display. The Sawyer-Massey Company had two big steam tractors and one gasoline unit in its exhibit. Likewise, the Case Company, an undisputed pioneer with steam tractors, was showing two steamers and one gasoline tractor. But other companies appeared to be betting on the internal combustion principle, the International Harvester Company, Fairbanks-Morse, and Big Four Company showing tractors with drive wheels of eight feet in diameter, and Rumely Company displaying two gasoline tractors, one of which would be presented as the prize for the best bushel of hard wheat in the big contests.

Present were some tractor innovations of historic note, among them a four-wheel-drive tractor called Olmstead, so new and so far ahead of its time that it was not attracting much attention. It was making history more than friends. And scarcely less novel were the Holt Caterpillar tractors, one of which was seen pulling a harvester-combine, giving Charlie Noble and many farmers like him their first chance to see such still controversial inventions.

The center of Congress interest was still in the grain show and the winners there. "Who will win the Rumely Oil-Pull?" was the question raised in scores of conversations. Some 200 entries of wheat were automatically in the competition, and Canadians could not restrain their joy when they heard that the Rumely would remain in Alberta and make its home on the farm of Henry Holmes of Raymond. Having won the supreme prize with his bushel of the new Marquis wheat, Holmes was winning the world championship for Canada for the second successive year. Just one year earlier, Seager Wheeler of Rosthern, Saskatchewan, gained fame by winning the world wheat crown, also with the new Canadian variety that was to extend the area of wheat production in the West and become the world hallmark of quality. The Wheeler success was at the New York Land Show of 1911 and was the beginning of a long succession of international wheat honors for western Canada.

Canadians were prominent among the winners in most of the grain classes at the Congress. A. Perry of Cardston won the Fairbanks-Morse gasoline engine and pumping gear for the best collection of grains and forages entered by an individual farmer. A. R. McFadden of Fort Macleod won the Northwest Harvester Company's road drag for the best essay on "Why It Pays Farmers To Build Good Roads." The Oliver gang plow for the best bushel of oats went to J. Lanigan from Elfros, Saskatchewan; the twenty-two-wheel packer donated by the International Harvester Company for the best peck of flax was won by H. Woolley, Dunmore, Alberta; and the Stewart sheaf loader, by R. H. Carter of Fort Qu'Appelle. The McCormick grain binder went to B. T. Bailey of Lacombe; the John Deere binder, to an exhibitor from Oregon; and the corn prize, to an exhibitor from Oklahoma.

Charlie Noble, with more than 5,000 acres of cultivated land including summerfallow at the time of the Congress gatherings, was busy enough trying to keep weeds down and get his crops harvested. He was not an exhibitor, but he was an eager visitor for as much time as he could spare away from his own operations. Other guests at the Congress soon recognized him as one of the biggest operators in the area, and he became a center of interest. As one who was still only nine years away from the point of taking a homestead, his record was recognized as a good success story. Visitors considering the purchase of farm lands in Canada sought his advice, knowing that he was the best authority on real estate as well as dry land farm practices.

Almost daily when driving back and forth over the twenty-mile road between Lethbridge and the Grand View Farm, he was transporting visitors who wanted to learn more about his operations and see where he had made the notable success with flax in that year, bringing him the well deserved title of Flax King of Alberta.

Probably Professor Bolley, speaking at Colorado Springs in the previous year, had inspired the idea of growing flax, but in any case, Noble went into the crop the way he went into most enterprises, in a big way. As the *Lethbridge Herald* told it: "He prepared the land, conserved the moisture and if there was any crop to be grown, he was bound to have it. . . . It is a safe bet that he will be found in the front seat at the meetings at the Dry Farming Congress where new ideas are to be picked up. This year he cultivated 3,000 acres and strange to relate, it wasn't wheat. He had only 80 acres sown to wheat. He put in 2,400 acres of flax and he had it all cut by September 14th. It threshed out an average of 20 bushels to the acre. Over 500 acres of oats threshed out 100 bushels to the acre."[3]

The flax recovery was described as an $81,000 crop, and it was something for the visitors to the Congress to ponder. They did, and Mr. Noble was asked to present a paper on his farming experiences in this semiarid region. He accepted the assignment, and the resulting paper was published later by the *Farm and Ranch Review*.[4]

Noble knew that as something to be shared with a dry farming audience, his dearly bought experiences in the drought year of 1910 and since that time would be most relevant. That dry year, he admitted, became an incentive to greater efforts in the pursuit of better farming. He made some mistakes then which he would not make again. By profiting from the mistakes and experiences of the dry year, he would make 1910 pay some unexpected dividends.

Dealing with the cropping program of the year in which he was speaking, he described the breaking of 1,370 acres of raw land in 1911, using the Reeves steam engine and a ten-furrow Cockshutt plow to which a heavy roller was attached to press the unruly sods into place. Thus, the turned furrows were left smooth and receptive to double discing and harrowing with horse-drawn implements.

Stanley wheat grown on part of this land in 1912 yielded thirty-seven bushels per acre. Another part of the same land was seeded to oats which yielded 107 bushels per acre, sufficient to impress any dry land farmer. At thirty-seven cents a bushel, Noble explained, the return from the oats was $33.32 per acre and thus more than the trading price of most farm land.

But it was the adventure with flax on a large scale that found the widest public interest, and Mr. Noble explained everything. The seeding of flax on new breaking began on April 17, at planting rates ranging from forty to fifty-five pounds per acre. Harvesting on this spread of 1,050 acres began on the last day of August, using ordinary binders equipped with flax attachments. The yield on the new breaking was an amazing twenty-five bushels to the acre.

Then, in addition to the flax seeded on the new land, Noble planted 1,400 acres on stubble land which had been burned over, then disced and harrowed. The practice of burning stubble was one which Mr. Noble roundly condemned later because of its tendency to invite soil drifting, but in that year of 1912, before soil erosion became prevalent, it resulted in the good return of twenty bushels of flax per acre. He added for the benefit of his audience that he did not intend to plant flax in the future except on summerfallowed land.

He had more to say about summerfallowing practices, much of it similar to what H. W. Campbell had been saying. The main purpose of summerfallowing was and always would be to save all possible moisture for the crop of the next year. During the season of 1912 he had summerfallowed 3,700 acres, using two Reeves steam tractors and several three-furrow plows pulled by ten-horse outfits. Plowing was at a depth of between seven and nine inches. Part of the purpose in plowing so deeply was to increase the moisture-holding capacity of the topsoil, and part was the hope of bringing some of the subsoil into the top layers. The plowing was followed by discing and harrowing, leaving the surface smooth and pulverized to a degree which even Mr. Noble would have frowned upon later when soil drifting became a widespread menace. Mr. Noble was one of the first to sense the drifting dangers, but at the time when he was speaking to the Congress group, his summerfallowing methods had the great merit of aiding the retention of the maximum amount of moisture.

He was speaking as a dry land farmer operating in a big way, but he was not necessarily recommending the large scale plan. He was honest and capable of being wholly objective. He had reservations about tractor power, even though he was a massive user of it at times.

"I have operated gasoline engines," he said, "but cannot feel friendly toward them. We have done exceptionally good work with steam, but in my opinion the engine power has been crowded upon the farmer to such an extent as to have the effect of getting land under cultivation more rapidly than labor and capital can be secured to work it properly."

In a sense it was self-criticism, something in which only big and humble people indulge. "We have often become too enthusiastic over our large yields, . . . getting into the way of doing things by excitement, in many cases overreaching our financial ability, and in some instances meeting with absolute failure where we should have had the best of success with smaller acreages."

Often during his life he spoke about the good lives people could have on smaller or average-sized farms. Sometimes he expressed envy of farmers on smaller holdings who could afford the traditional farm freedom without the cares of the big operator. But there seemed to be within him an inherent attraction for big farms, and he did not resist.

His listeners on that Congress occasion knew they were in the presence of a man of honesty and frankness. "While I am operating on a rather large scale," he said, "I am certain that by taking more pride in doing a smaller amount of farming in the best way and raising the best possible grade of livestock, we [can] increase the value of our land more rapidly, as well as our net gain in farming operations."

"More attention should be given to small things," he was saying while his friends knew that thinking small and working small were activities which the speaker would never find it easy to perform.

His final observations would confirm the quality of his farming ideals: "In harmony with our objectives, we shall naturally give more attention to the growing of trees and the beautifying of our homes, all of which will react in a way to help us set a better example for our growing boys and to afford us more of the real pleasures of the most independent of callings."[5]

Charles Noble admitted that he had gained much from the hours spent at the sixth — and perhaps best — annual gathering of the International Dry Farming Congress, but it was no less evident that he had contributed to it, substantially.

8
THE NOBLE FOUNDATION

Charles Noble's enterprise continued to grow like an over-stuffed gosling. In 1913 — the tenth anniversary of his entry upon the quarter section homestead at Claresholm and the tenth anniversary of his marriage — nearly all of the twelve sections of semiarid prairie land over which he presided were in a state of cultivation. In Charlie Noble's case, that meant good cultivation, about as nearly weedless as it was possible to have it. Of the 7,574 cultivated acres, summerfallow accounted for 2,845 acres or about one third of the total, and the seeded portion was divided; 2,880 acres in oats, 1,186 acres in wheat, 462 in barley, and 200 in flax.[1]

Big farms could never escape big operating expenses for hired help, seed grain, machinery and machinery repairs, feed for horses or fuel for tractors, capital charges, and a multitude of unforeseen items, and financing was often difficult. Finding the needed funds in the spring of 1913 was particularly memorable. A line of credit for $19,000 at a Lethbridge bank was depleted before seeding began. The banker, who was well aware of the big capital debt clinging to the land the way a hawk clings to a protesting mouse, said with the conclusiveness of an aging school teacher: "No more."

It was an extremely awkward situation, and Noble knew that arguing with a banker was about as futile as arguing with a doctor who says you have mumps. But the farmer had to get the seed in the ground by one means or another, and after exploring other avenues of hope, he boarded a train going to Devil's Lake, North Dakota, where friends of other years had not forgotten him and would still trust him with a loan. According to his own telling, he returned with his pockets bulging with cash, enough to insure completion of seeding.

But as if to justify the banker's fears, 1913 turned out to be another dry year — just 14.17 inches of precipitation for the full twelve months at Lethbridge. Fortunately, however, a substantial part of the season's rain fell at the time when it could be most effective, and coupled with the fortune of good timing in rains was the fact of the summerfallowed land being worked with typical Noble care for the capture and retention of all possible moisture from the previous year. The result was a surprisingly good crop. The Banner oats from the summerfallowed land yielded 102 bushels per acre, and the Marquis wheat from Seager Wheeler seed returned 40 bushels per acre.

On September 29 of that year, according to a published account, fifty-nine freight cars loaded with grain from the Noble farms "were on the road between Lethbridge and Fort William," while back at home there was still "a private elevator with 60,000 bushels and many field bins loaded, including one full of oats that measured 100 by 16 by 10 feet high."[2] It meant that the equivalent of a train load of Noble's grain was on its way to market and an amount equal to another train load was still on the farm. From the stores remaining, close to eighty-five carloads of Banner oats were shipped for seed purposes.

The friends at Devil's Lake were promptly repaid, with thanks. Likewise, outstanding operating expenses were paid in full although the creditors looking for interest and installment money on the land purchases did not get the full amounts as set down in the agreements. Within the next year, there was another financial crisis.

It seemed to be the common lot of big farm operators to be rich in capital assets and poor in liquid assets. Noble's real estate wealth in 1913 was said to be above $300,000, and yet he was in arrears on payments of both principal and interest to the Oregon estate from which he had bought the Grand View land. The trouble traced to that $80,000 obligation to the McCormick estate which had grown rather than decreased. The combination of dry years and the seventy-five-cents-per-bushel wheat explained why the debt, with interest, had climbed to about $100,000. To have made the prescribed land payments would have been just too much for the already overtaxed returns from the 1913 crop, and the creditors instructed their Alberta lawyer, Hector H. Gilchrist of the Calgary law firm of Aitkin, Gilchrist, and O'Rourke, to investigate and advise about foreclosure proceedings.

An account of the lawyer's handling of the case was saved for posterity by a series of circumstances that brought the story to the well known western journalist Leonard Nesbitt. The lawyer, who later became a close personal friend of Mr. Noble, chose to live after his retirement at Owen Sound in Ontario. During his years in that attractive community clinging to the south shore of Georgian Bay, Gilchrist wrote a few sketches about western people he had known, among them Charles S. Noble. Copies of some of these were given to Mr. Gilchrist's Owen Sound neighbor Mrs. Fred Edmonds, who in turn sent them to her brother Leonard Nesbitt in Alberta. Mr. Nesbitt then shared the lawyer's reminiscences in an article written for the *Brooks Bulletin* with which he had a long editorial association.

In the discharge of his instructions, Mr. Gilchrist visited Nobleford on a June day and was driven to all parts of the farms. "Mr. Noble," Gilchrist wrote, "took me all over the ten thousand acres in an old Ford car and we took down what he said [about] wheat, oats, and barley. We stood in the midst of thousands of acres of beautifully summerfallowed land. It all looked like a [good] garden. There was not a weed of any kind or size to be seen anywhere."

Mr. Gilchrist continued: "As I caught the C.P.R. train to Calgary in the evening, I walked down the station platform with Mr. Noble and he asked: 'What's it going to be young man?'

"I replied: 'You are the best damn farmer I have ever seen in my life and if this land is any good, you will surely pay for it. I intend to write Judge Lee and tell him to give you every chance.'

Gratefully, Mr. Noble replied: 'Just tell him to give me that chance and I will pay up.' "3

The chance was given, and the payments were made with as much regularity as the circumstances of yield and the price of grain would allow.

Western farms of 5,000 or 10,000 acres never failed to become centers of special public interest, rather commonly a critical interest. Neglected fences and thin horses and patches of sow thistle might be sympathetically overlooked on the ordinary farm of average size, but not on the big one. Neighbors were likely to make jokes about extravagances and mistakes and speculate about how long the big spreads would last. The best target for jokes was the company-owned farm or the big operation of a nonresident proprietor. The big farms were fine in theory, but most of them did not last very long and in their short spans of existence, seemed to furnish more public entertainment than either inspiration or leadership or dividends.

But such general rules did not apply to the Noble farms. One who was a neighbor during the period of the First World War said quite seriously: "We'd have laughed too if we had seen something to laugh about. But when the man running the big show was getting better yields and had fewer weeds than the rest of us, we were too busy trying to figure it out to laugh."

Perhaps it was because of mistakes more than triumphs, but in any case, many of the farms of supersize became enshrined in pioneer memories. One of the first of those titanic farms was that of the Qu'Appelle Valley Farming Company — better known as the Major Billy Bell Farm — at Indian Head. Initially it comprised a block of about one hundred square miles, except for a couple of small places held by unyielding squatters. Some of the furrows cut by walking plows in that first year of operations, 1882, were reported to be ten miles long, indicating that horses and plowmen starting at one end of the huge property in the morning could hope to be at the far end of the furrow for the noontime pause and back at the starting point at quitting time in the evening, having made one round of twenty miles during the day.

Bell had a spectacular year in 1884, sending forty-five "self-binders" of the newest kind to the fields at harvest time. Seven steam-driven threshing machines did the threshing and turned out 130,000 bushels of grain, much of it badly frozen. But successes were matched by costly reverses, and the glory of the Bell Farm was brief.

Then there was the widely publicized string of big farms and ranches, the property of the Canadian Agricultural, Coal and Colonization Company, founded with English capital by the irrepressible little Englishman Sir John Lister Kaye in 1887. Sir John liked big and round figures and tailored his plan around ten properties of 10,000 acres each spotted along the main line of the CPR, between Balgonie on the east and Langdon on the west. To stock these farm and ranch spreads with breeding herds, Sir John bought 7,000 Powder River Ranch cattle carrying the brand "76." That purchase explained why the big place became known by the brand name "The 76."

Sir John announced his intention of bringing 50,000 sheep from the United States but settled for a smaller number, 10,000. At the same time, he was breaking up several thousand acres of land for wheat, some of it in the driest part of the West. When crops failed because of drought, the amazing Sir John resolved to irrigate his big expanse of wheat land by the use of forty-four pine tanks made in Winnipeg in 1889. Each tank was eleven feet four inches long, three feet seven inches wide, and two feet high. A full tank would hold about twelve barrels, but when it is realized that it would take more than a hundred tons of water to furnish just one inch of irrigation on a single acre, the utter futility of the exercise will be appreciated.

Again, the errors in judgment were especially costly to a big farm, and when deficits soared, Sir John retired from the prairie scene and went back to England. His biggest contribution to western agriculture was in making blunders that wise observers would not repeat.

Even in Mr. Noble's generation, he was not the only one attempting to farm in a big and handsome way. There were the Andrew Anderson farm at Alsask, the Detchon farm at Davidson, and the Fred Engen farm on the Goose Lake line southwest of Saskatoon. The last was of special interest because of similarities between Engen and Noble. Both came from North Dakota in the same year; both suffered setbacks; both harvested spectacular flax crops worth about $80,000 in 1912. Engen, by that year, had more land than Noble and had gone in for power farming to a greater extent. In the autumn of 1912, he had three Big Four tractors, each pulling six binders in one field, cutting a swath that would be 144 feet in width. The story never told was how often the six binders were brought to a stop because of a mechanical disorder in one of them.

Suffield, northwest of Medicine Hat, was the setting for the monster Canadian Wheatlands Limited farm, big enough in its 66,000 acres of raw land to overshadow the Charles Noble venture, at least in area. But the two farms were not really comparable. The Suffield land being broken and cultivated by means of five steam tractors, three Marshall gasoline tractors, and a varying number of single-furrow plows drawn by oxen was in a state of preparation to receive irrigation water and be ready for sale in small parcels to colonists from the United Kingdom.

Twelve thousand acres were broken in 1911, and the intention was to break a similar amount in 1912. With operations being supervised by James Murray, who was later employed as superintendent for Charlie Noble, the technique followed in breaking consisted of shallow plowing in June or July, then discing and backsetting at a depth of six inches.

The gigantic Wheatlands scheme was initiated by J. D.

McGregor of the famous Glencarnock Farms at Brandon, whose herd of Aberdeen Angus cattle furnished the steer, Glencarnock Victor, which brought fame to western Canada as well as the breeder and owner by winning the grand championship in fat cattle classes at the International Fat Stock Show at Chicago in 1912. It was the most coveted honor to be won at that great show, and the McGregor success was something to rival the Seager Wheeler championship for wheat in the previous year. And with McGregor as with Wheeler, it was not the only triumph of its kind; he went back the next year and gained the same high international honor with another black steer, Glencarnock Victor II.

If McGregor's farming scheme on the Alberta prairie had been carried through, it might have made a big impression upon western Canadian agriculture. But war in Europe interfered with the program, and the farm never did fulfill its intended purpose. Many of the irrigation canals never carried water, and many of the cultivated lands were never occupied by settlers. Wheatlands Limited and the Noble farms had practically nothing in common except that both were big. One of the enterprises lived on to become a lasting force in the agricultural community, and the other did not.

Being big in the farming business has always been fascinating to some people, but it was never easy or safe. As the size of a farm doubled, it seemed, the risks were trebled or quadrupled. Charlie Noble, although drawn instinctively to large scale operations in anything he undertook was the first to admit that size alone was an inadequate goal. The challenge in a big farm was in making it a good farm.

And farms, like the people who operated them, should have had a recognizable individuality. Whether big or small, by Charlie Noble's reasoning, farms were entitled to be useful in different ways. If the big farm enterprise was not demonstrating something positive and useful in the production of human food, it would be better for its owner to have a small farm or no farm at all.

It was the concept of responsibility and service that brought the Noble Foundation into existence. It was something completely new, an adventure in agricultural idealism. Regardless of its success, it was enough in itself to give the Noble farm a striking individuality, to make it a big farm with a clear difference.

In creating the Foundation, Charlie Noble had the valuable assistance of his brother Newell James Noble, the oldest of six

boys in the family and a year and a half older than Charlie.
Newell James fared better than Charlie in getting an education,
and after teaching school in North Dakota and doing a stint of
service in the Spanish-American War, he attended university in
North Dakota and graduated in law. It was then, in 1913, that
Charles Noble persuaded his brother to join him in Alberta.
There Newell James left an imprint upon the Noble farms in
general and the Foundation in particular.

He was much like his brother in many ways, being six feet
two inches tall, spare, and mentally active, but more idealistic
and less practical. As noted by his nephew Shirley Noble, "N. J.
was a great admirer of Abraham Lincoln and read all the
Lincolniana he could secure. He followed the Lincoln tradition
of plain and simple living, and most of his spare time was given
to searching out what he termed the 'fundamentals' of such
widely varying subjects as mechanical design, monetary reform,
philosophy, and religion. In physical stature at least, he bore a
slight resemblance to the great President and I believe he
strived to imitate him in other respects."[4]

The organization and incorporation of the Noble Foundation
were assignments that suited Newell James Noble perfectly,
and a prospectus appeared in October, 1913, just at the time the
hamlet of Noble was being formally renamed Nobleford. The
public announcement bore a strong moral tone with an
expression of sincerity that nobody could question. The
opening statement declared that: "The Noble Foundation,
Limited, is laid on the belief that the world has outgrown its
present business methods, that in civilized nations at least, the
time has come when poverty may and should be abolished, that
the present regime, however well it may have been adapted to
conditions one hundred years ago, has, on account of the great
progress the world has made since then, become instead of a
help a hindrance and a real menace to all our cherished
institutions, that it promotes greed and gambling instead of
thrift and honesty, and that it is one of the fundamental causes
of the movement toward the cities, and the consequent
deterioration of the soil, which some economists declare is the
real cause of race decadence. It is founded on the further belief
that a wise direction of forces still within our control will
eventually establish a new regime vastly superior in every
respect and capable of giving to every worthy man a worthy
place in life."

It was not the kind of message generally expected from those
who directed supersized farms or any other big operation. But

there it was: "The purpose of the Noble Foundation is to provide a means whereby any honest, hardworking man or woman may begin life with an assurance of the greatest usefulness and the highest degree of success.... The plan is intended at the same time to provide a perfectly safe place for the investment of capital. In a word, it is intended to recast business methods in a way to secure the greatest efficiency and economy in every respect, and thus to lead the way to a final abolition of poverty."[5]

How was this glorious scheme "to unite labor and capital in a way that they have never been united before," to be carried out? At first there were to be two companies, the holding company to be known as the Noble Foundation, Limited, and a subsidiary, the Noble Seed and Live Stock Company, Limited. The latter was not pursued, and the foundation became the body to which the company employees could subscribe. Workmen who demonstrated an interest in permanent employment could buy shares in the company by paying ten per cent of the purchase price and signing a note for the balance. The company would then advance the balance of payment and expect to recover the amount of the advance from authorized wage deductions and from dividends earned by the shares. The employee could thus acquire substantial holdings in shares with relatively small cash payments.

As an illustration advanced by Newell James, the employee who contracted to buy fifty shares at $100 each at the beginning of the year would pay ten per cent or $500 at the outset. Interest at eight per cent on the unpaid balance of $4,500 would be $360 for the year, but payments from wage deductions at $20 per month would reduce the indebtedness by $240 and the presumed dividend of fifteen per cent on fifty shares would further reduce the debt by $750. Hence, the employee who purchased $5,000 worth of shares at the beginning of the year would have reduced his debt to $3,870 in the first year and to $3,189.60 by the end of the second year.[6]

The announcements were cheerful. The prospects were bright because the big Noble enterprise was a going concern. To the question "Who is behind this proposition and what are his assets?" the answer as set down was "C. S. Noble, who owns this and other land, is worth $330,000 above liabilities." To another question "Is the property on a paying basis at present?" the reply was "Yes, profits were eleven per cent in 1912 when oats yielded 107½ bushels per acre; wheat, 36 bushels; flax, 27½ bushels." Fifteen per cent dividend was anticipated for 1913, with dividends rising to twenty per cent in later years.

In the opinion of its creators, the scheme offered aspiring young farmers more than homesteading, more than renting, and more than buying on crop payments. It would also, the Nobles believed, insure the best care of farms, especially the soil. "The main difficulty with corporation farming on a large scale," the company report stated, "seems to be the lack of interest in the success of the business on the part of those doing the work." Perchance it did explain why so many of the large farming concerns were terminated too soon. In contrast, the Foundation plan would "be distinguished from ordinary farming corporations and from landlordism by the fact that the laborers [would gain] a complete interest in the property and thus enhance instead of destroy the advantages pertaining to large management."

As if to justify the idealistic hope, the workers did respond by buying shares. It made no less work and responsibility for Charlie Noble, but it made him happy.

Here, indeed, was another side of this complex fellow. People working close to him thought they understood him. They saw him as a man of exceptional drive, rarely relaxed, friendly but not overly warm. They knew that his alarm clock was the first in the municipality to sound in the morning and that he scarcely stopped until bedtime at night, often depriving himself of meals and sleep. Of course, he was ambitious and restless like a racehorse in a starting gate. He seemed incapable of finding a place to pause for a recess. Having bought one farm, he was immediately thinking about another until he had Mountain View, Grand View, Marquis, Prairie Grange, Fraser, and Cameron, and neighbors, thinking they saw something resembling a toboggan gathering momentum as it raced down a hillside, enquried: "Where will this mad drive end?"

That side of the great and honest Charles Noble became pretty well known. What was not so well known was his idealism, as fresh and vibrant as the sentiment in Lincoln's speech at Gettysburg. The formation of the Foundation spoke more loudly than words. As another instrument for making money, the Foundation was not needed. It had no really practical function, but in carrying out an ideal, it did not fail and showed Charlie Noble's high and honest motives. It too fell upon troubled times, but it was still able to draw the judgment that in principle it was the finest fruit to come from any of western Canada's colossal farms.

9
PATRIOTISM AND PRODUCTION

As a crop year, 1915 had everything in its favor — rain when needed, relative freedom from pests, an ideal harvest season, heavy yields in almost all parts of the country, and ready markets with rising prices for everything growers had to sell. To farmers who had been tormented by crop reverses in a score of forms, it seemed too good to be true, and they did not forget it. Men who were guilty of forgetting the respective years in which they were married or who no longer remembered their wives' birthdays recalled 1915 as the year of the big crop and a holiday trip to California.

The three midwestern provinces produced 360 million bushels of wheat, averaging 26 bushels per acre. About two thirds of that output was Marquis, making 1915 the first big year for the relatively new variety. Such production had not happened before and would not happen again for many years. To Charlie Noble, it was "the year that left farmers with nothing about which to complain except sore backs from shovelling wheat."

The crop returns were so good that the editor of the *Lethbridge Herald*, on the first day of November when most farm promissory notes came due, proposed a province-wide Farmers' Festival. It was to be partly along the lines of the Dry Farming Congress of 1912 and partly like a special Thanksgiving. The idea was a worthy one but most people were too busy to pursue it.

To make it still more memorable, it was the first full year of World War I, bringing anxiety and added burdens along with the farm successes. For Canadians and all citizens of the Empire, the long and brutal and costly struggle began when Britain declared war on Germany on August 4, 1914. By the beginning of 1915, the full and awful impact was being felt across the entire country, no less in wheat growing areas than elsewhere. Men of the first Canadian contingent — 33,000 of them — were sailing to England just over two months after war was declared and entering the trenches on the Western Front in February.

In the meantime, while the supremacy of Britain's surface fleet was being confirmed in naval battle, its helplessness in preventing the enemy's ruthless submarine attacks upon shipping in all forms — merchant ships and passenger ships as well as naval vessels — was also being demonstrated. The German aim, as declared at the beginning of February, 1915, was to employ naval blockade to starve Britain into surrender. By sinking a million tons of shipping per month, it was calculated, the hunger-induced surrender would come in less than six months.

Carriers of all sizes and kinds on the shipping lanes to Britain and France became targets for torpedoes, and even some passenger liners were sent to the bottom of the Atlantic, with high loss of life. The *Lusitania*, one of the finest and fastest ships afloat, was torpedoed by a submarine off the coast of Ireland on May 7, 1915, with the loss of 1,198 men, women, and children.

One of the important casualties was grain from Canada, and it was not long before the danger of critical food shortages in Britain and Allied countries was recognized. For the millions of people overseas who were relying upon Canadian grain, there remained only two possible solutions — first, the destruction of the offending submarines, and second, the delivery of such larger-than-normal amounts that they would compensate for losses at sea and declines in home production in war-torn countries. Efforts to destroy the submarines were not effective, leaving an increase in the production and shipping of Canadian grains as the only reasonable alternative.

For people like Charlie Noble, the message needed no amplification. He was a grain-growing specialist, forty-two years of age and in the best possible position to make his contribution to a country at war. For any who did not get the message about mounting needs for wheat and other agricultural products, there was the clear call from Hon. Martin Burrell, Canada's minister of agriculture, urging greater production:

"Approximately twenty-five million men have been mobilized in Europe," he said. "A large proportion of these have been drawn from the farms of the countries at war. Even in neutral countries, large numbers of food producers have been called from the land to be ready for emergencies. . . . These millions [called for service] cease to be producers . . . worse still, they have become destroyers of food."

Canadians were not hesitating in what they saw as their duty, sending trained men to stand with overseas allies and furnishing needed supplies in any shape or form. They were ready to conform obediently to all orders dictated by war. In their patriotism, they were uncompromising. Even neighbors with German names were looked upon with suspicion, and the one making a few indiscreet remarks might find himself in an internment camp.

With so much emphasis on production, farmers gained instant prestige, and church ministers, members of parliament, and editors went out of their way to make flattering remarks. The president of the Lethbridge Board of Trade said the war had served to show how "the world as a whole lives from hand-to-mouth," making the farmer paramount in times of either peace or war.[2] A high ranking railroad official, not wishing to be outdone in popular praise for farming, said that training in agriculture should be a prerequisite for all aspiring members of parliament.[3]

As producers of food, farmers had always been important, but now the urgency seemed greater and they were hearing the plea to produce more both from more acres and from more per acre. Charlie Noble more than anybody could tell how it could be done, and in the next few years he conducted the clearest demonstrations of how it was being done. His land had always produced well above the average, offering the most convincing proof that all soils would respond to better care and better cultivation. Now, in wartime, his voice and leadership were needed more than ever.

Departments of agriculture, both provincial and federal, called conferences for the purpose of promoting greater production. When the dominion's professionals in agriculture like W. H. Fairfield, who was superintendent of the nearby experimental station, and E. S. Archibald, who was destined to become the director of Canada's experimental farm system, appeared to face a big audience of farming people at Lethbridge on March 6, they asked Charlie Noble to join them as a conference speaker. They knew him as the big farmer who had

achieved spectacular success in overcoming dry farming problems and were perfectly right in presuming that his message
would be well received.

Ever willing to help in a good cause, Noble agreed and met
an appreciative audience. His manner was unprofessional but
his words were practical. He reminded his listeners that
Canada's best wheat and most of Canada's wheat came from
this semiarid part of the West. It was not a region that would
ever offer easy or risk-free farming. Natural hazards would
create difficulties but farmers could do much to minimize
losses. They could not stop the hail, he noted, but they could
take out hail insurance. They could not prevent early fall frosts,
but they could choose earlier maturing crop varieties possessing better chances of missing the frosts. They could not escape
years of extreme drought, but they could and should be diligent
in conserving moisture by destroying the moisture-robbing
weeds and employing summerfallow. If the latter were prepared
with proper care, farmers could be practically assured of a fair
crop on at least half of their land every year.

The speaker had more to say about the correct way of
summerfallowing. It was a subject that had engaged his studied
interest for years, and nobody was in a better position to offer
advice about it. Standing straight and tall, with his hands deep
in his pockets, he warmed to his subject, recommending
starting the summerfallow by using the disc on stubble land,
right after the binder in the autumn, and plowing deeply in the
spring. Deep plowing would insure a bigger reservoir for
moisture. Under some circumstances he would recommend the
use of a packer after the plow, but in any case, each day's
plowing should be harrowed during the same day to form a
mulch, one more step in preventing loss of the precious
moisture by evaporation. And, of course, all weed growth
should be prevented.

It was his favorite theme, and then he had some advice about
wind erosion which had not yet become common enough to be
seen as a serious danger. "If the soil particles become too dry so
that the winds carry them off, a spring-toothed [cultivator] just
after a rain will leave the soil in lumps large enough to
overcome the drifting."[4]

Sixty years later, such advice about the prevention or control
of soil drifting seemed primitive, but having regard for the
limited experience from which men of 1915 could draw, nobody
had anything better to offer and Noble became one of the first
Canadians to talk from a platform about the impending menace.

Holding his audience like a seasoned campaigner, this man whose formal education ended at grade eight made a strong case for mixed farming and then advised that "every farmer should keep a complete set of books so he can tell at any season of the year just what his operations are costing him."

Finally, in making a plea for more intensive care in handling soil and in all aspects of farming, he made what some observers thought was a confession, admitting that: "We have been farming on too large a scale," adding that he did not think it was due to greed but rather to the manner in which people thought they had to farm dry land.[5]

In his admission about "farming on too large a scale," Noble may have sounded somewhat like Bob Edwards of Calgary "Eye Opener" fame. Edwards was at that very moment giving his approval and editorial support to the cause of prohibition as Albertans prepared for the July plebiscite, a giant test between the "wets" and the "drys" in the province. Bob was serious, but as his readers knew very well, he found it nigh impossible to apply the prohibition principle to his own life.

The dominion government's professionals in the science of agriculture, Archibald and Fairfield, were going on to other farming communities for similar conferences and were wise enough to ask Charlie Noble to accompany them and present his message to other groups of dry land farmers. And the man from Nobleford, although one of the busiest people in the southwest, agreed to go.

The humble fellow with a retiring manner had never thought of himself as a teacher or public speaker or educator, but a new role as an adviser on farm matters was appearing. Farmers would listen to another farmer more readily than to what some described derisively as "white collar agriculturists." Noble on the platform spoke in the simple farm terms and voice he would have used when standing in a field of summerfallow.

But agricultural education was coming to the fore. The province of Manitoba led the way in the West by establishing in 1906 an agricultural college, patterned after the Ontario Agricultural College in being placed "a safe distance" from the university. Saskatchewan was next and broke with Canadian tradition by placing the agricultural college at the very heart of the new university. Then Noble's province of Alberta sought to gain "the best of both worlds" by providing two levels of agricultural education, adopting the University of Saskatchewan plan of establishing a faculty of agriculture within the university and, at the same time, providing agricultural schools at country points for the accommodation of young farmers who were not within reach of high schools or whose high school deficiencies prevented university entrance. The schools of agriculture, dedicated to the betterment of young people returning to farms, were the Honorable Duncan Marshall's pride and joy and were constituted to be the responsibility of the provincial Department of Agriculture. Three of them — at Olds, Vermilion, and Claresholm — opened their doors to students in 1913.

Other Alberta points, including Lethbridge, wanted provincial schools of agriculture, and there was danger of overextending them and allowing them to become drawn into politics. A nonpolitical board of agricultural education was needed and was formed in 1916 with Charles S. Noble being named to sit with P. W. Warner of Edmonton, A. E. Shuttleworth of Blackie, and Lewis Hutchinson of Duhamel.[6]

Having made his debut as an unpaid public worker at farm conferences, Charlie Noble returned home in haste to prepare for seeding about 4,500 acres and summerfallowing as much more. While the seed was going into the ground, he would find time, he promised, to support and assist the campaign to make Alberta a prohibition province after the plebiscite on July 22. Noble was an uncompromising teetotaller, and the decisive victory on that day of the vote pleased him greatly. The only disappointing area was his own business center of Lethbridge, the only one of the Alberta cities that failed to give the "drys" a majority.

Seeding began with all the usual uncertainties of either a farming operation or a horse race, and before long there were the familiar indications of a dry season. But Mother Nature was teasing the growers as the "Old Lady" had done many times. The total precipitation for the calendar year at Lethbridge was only 17.27 inches, an amount that would not normally be conducive to a bumper crop. But again the point was made that the timing of the rains in relation to the growing season was fully as important as the total fall. As if directed by a master hand working to insure the grain supplies needed for wartime export, the rains fell when the crops needed them and could make the best use of them.

When seeding was completed, Mr. Noble could report 836 acres of wheat, 3,091 acres of oats, 390 acres of greenfeed, 75 acres of flax, and 70 acres of winter rye — also 50 experimental acres of alfalfa. The total ground seeded was 4,512 rather dry acres. In addition to the huge amount of plowing and packing and harrowing involved on the seeded land, there was the summerfallow, 4,170 acres of it.

The outlook was not favorable until mid-May brought that two-day, two-inch rain for which farmers had always hoped and prayed. The crops responded like an indolent hired man responding to a dinner bell, and record yields began to appear as possibilities.

A new problem loomed, that of obtaining sufficient help for the harvest. The combined effect of recruiting and attractive wages in munitions plants left many farmers wondering where they would find stookers and how they could make up crews for threshing, especially with a heavy crop. Fewer men would be coming west on that famous annual adventure, the harvesters' excursion. But it was arranged that soldiers in uniform might, under some circumstances, qualify for leave of absence to help in the harvest fields. The supply of workers was still inadequate, but strange as it seemed, the situation on the big Noble farm was less acute than on many smaller places because of the particularly good relations existing between the proprietor and the workmen. Many of the Noble helpers were permanent employees who appreciated the security and company benefits like wage bonus payments and the opportunity of acquiring shares in the Foundation.

With four big threshing machines in operation, the fields were clear on the central farm by late October, at which time the tiny hamlet of Nobleford could claim the distinction of being the biggest shipping point in terms of bushels of grain in all of southern Alberta. By the middle of October, the shipments totalled 220,000 bushels, most of which was from the Noble Foundation fields.

The farm's record-breaking crop of 1915 was oats, and over 300,000 bushels were threshed from the 3,091 acres planted, making for a general average of 100 bushels per acre. A measured area of 1,000 acres returned 126 bushels per acre, and a 100-acre field listed as a "plot" made 130 bushels to the acre. Writers for farm magazines hailed Mr. Noble as "the Oats King of Western Canada."

It was a big and notable year for the grain fields of the West, and many people were saying, "We won't see its equal again." But for Charlie Noble's farming enterprise, 1916 was a bigger one, especially with wheat.

The war situation had changed only slightly. Canada's forces in uniform had risen to almost 500,000 men. The great naval Battle of Jutland sent the German ships to cover, but the

German submarines were as dangerous and destructive as ever. People who dared to peer into the future believed there might be a 500 million bushel drop in North American grain production in the current year, with an increasing chance of serious world famine at war's end. There could be no relaxation in the drive for maximum production of food products. Western farmers were doing their best and making money at it. They knew they had very little about which to complain except the shortage of labor. The price of wheat which stood at eighty-four cents at Winnipeg at the beginning of war reached the two-dollar mark in November of 1916.

The crop sensation of the year was Charlie Noble's wheat, most of which was Marquis grown from registered seed bought from Seager Wheeler in 1913. Most of western Canada's wheat crop was not so fortunate in escaping trouble. The crop that started well in the spring and enjoyed ample moisture received a surprise setback in August. The destroyer this time was black rust, of which western farmers knew very little. The disease had appeared in Manitoba and Saskatchewan in 1904 and 1911, but the attacks were not heavy and nobody was greatly disturbed. Farmers were told by authorities who shared the growers' ignorance of the disease to burn their stubble and straw butts as a means of destroying surviving rust spores.

But 1916 was not like 1911; the disease struck earlier in southern Manitoba and southeastern Saskatchewan and reached a bigger area. Farmers were helpless as they watched otherwise good crops reduced to little more than straw. Their losses — mainly in Manitoba and Saskatchewan — were estimated at roughly 200 million dollars. But the costly encounter won the wholehearted attention of plant scientists and led to a coordinated attack upon the disease and to the ultimate production of new varieties possessing the high milling qualities of Marquis and the rust resistance of other kinds.

Traces of the rust were detected at Magrath and Lethbridge in early August, but southern Alberta managed to escape with only slight crop damage and thereby became an important source of seed for farms in the disaster areas. The Noble Foundation crops were pounded by a storm on August 9, but they recovered completely and Charles Noble began to sense yields of record proportions.

Cora Hind, agricultural editor for the *Winnipeg Free Press* and author of that paper's internationally famous crop reports, came that way in late August and saw the best stands of grain she had encountered on her tour. Going from Nobleford to

Calgary, she sent a telegram message to her paper, telling that:
"Southern Alberta has a magnificent crop of all grains,
especially wheat and given until September 15 without frost,
will harvest the largest quantity of high grade wheat in its
history, not excepting the bumper year of 1915."[7]

Miss Hind was right in her judgment of the southern Alberta
crop, and the best of southern Alberta may have been what she
saw on the Noble Foundation farms. Some amazing wheat yield
records were established in the previous year, but now there
was speculation that the stand of wheat on one of Mr. Noble's
big fields might outscore all previous records for big areas.
People of the region were probably feeling some depression
from the continuous stream of war news — much of it bad news
— and when the *Lethbridge Herald* reported the speculation
about the possibility of a world record being made in a
Nobleford wheat field, public interest mounted as it might be
expected to soar in an election.

World records are the best of materials for publicity and
could be good for business. Noble's neighbors, harboring no
jealousy, were among the first to show enthusiasm, and the
Lethbridge Herald did a first class job of whipping up urban
emotion. For days after September 28, the newspaper carried
front page reports about threshing progress at Nobleford,
especially on the 1,000 acres of carefully measured ground from
which a world record for such a large area loomed. The editor
called it "The Race For The World's Record" in the class for
big fields. Even the World Series in baseball, which was in
progress at the same time, had to share front page space with
the news from Nobleford.

J. W. McClean of Monarch had established a southern
Alberta record for a large wheat acreage when he threshed an
average of fifty-two bushels per acre on 1,440 acres in 1915.
That would be hard to beat, but an even higher hope in the
district was that the Noble crop would surpass the acknowledged world record of fifty-three bushels per acre claimed by a
dry land grower in Colfax County in the state of Washington.

Mr. Noble, ever on the best of terms with the business people
of Lethbridge, entered readily into the fun and enthusiasm
being generated in Lethbridge and invited the mayor, members
of the council, members and friends of the board of trade, and
others who showed an interest to visit the farm on the day
when, by his calculation, the threshing on the thousand
measured acres would be brought to conclusion.

There was a threshing delay because of a spell of snow and

rain but operations resumed, and the big outing at the farm, like an adventure in rural-urban relations, was fixed for October 25. The daily paper did well in maintaining a state of public suspense to the last. It was reported on the front page that the first 469 acres of the good crop yielded fifty-two bushels per acre. That would not be high enough to qualify as a world record but still there was hope. The next report revealed that the average yield on the larger area of 631 acres threshed was unchanged at fifty-two bushels per acre. The chance of an international record seemed to be diminishing but interest was not.

The organized cavalcade of automobiles — practically all the cars in Lethbridge — lined up on the street in front of the board of trade office for an orderly departure at a stated hour. It was the biggest collection of cars seen in southern Alberta, with 150 citizens as eager passengers. Some of the guests had come from a distance. Governments and the CPR were officially represented. Mr. Noble's old friend and partner T. C. Milnes came from Claresholm. Many local schools were dismissed for the day, and numerous country neighbors joined the parade at convenient points along the twenty-mile road. An editor said the excitement was "like a Fourth of July celebration on the Arizona frontier. . . ." Nobody was disappointed.

As the press reported it: "The last load of the record crop was drawn to the machine in the presence of Mr. Noble himself, Mayor Hardie and President Marnoch of the Lethbridge Board of Trade, officials of the Department of Natural Resources of the C.P.R., and other visitors to a considerable number."[8]

Finally, when all the weights were assembled and totalled, Mr. Noble's 1,000 measured acres had yielded 54,395 bushels of wheat, or an average of fifty-four bushels and twenty-three pounds per acre, surpassing the world's best known record for a thousand acres or more.[9] A movie camera, an instrument which most people had not seen before, was present to capture in picture the last load of the golden grain on its way to the elevator.

Somebody said that the elevator weights would have shown a still higher yield if the visitors had not been so eager to fill their pockets with souvenir samples of the widely publicized wheat.

Anyway, it was a proud tribute to a man and to the potential of properly cultivated western soil, performing without irrigation and without artificial fertilizer. And great was the rejoicing. It was enough to overshadow the Boston Americans' four to one victory over the Brooklyn Nationals in the final game of the World Series. And the reception and good farm food furnished by Mr. and Mrs. Noble were in keeping with the festive spirit of the day when the people of Lethbridge participated in a friendly invasion of the Noble farming empire.

What the urban people saw that day was far more than the concluding chapter in the winning of a world title: They saw how a mammoth farm operated; they saw three threshing machines being driven by three big steamer tractors on one farm; they saw three stook loaders elevating stooks to the big bundle racks to be drawn to the threshing machines by four-horse teams; they saw fifty-three workmen and about a hundred horses and mules going steadily to keep the threshing outfits operating to capacity. It was not just to make a yield record but rather to recover the wheat from 1,800 acres and the oats and other grains from about 3,000 acres, all of which would be needed urgently, some for seed in the neighboring provinces where stem rust had been a 1916 destroyer, some for milling to meet Canadian demands, some for feed to insure supplies of livestock products in Canadian diets, and some for export to Britain and Britain's allies.

It was a memorable day for the visitors from Lethbridge and elsewhere, as it was a memorable year for the man who was called the Flax King in 1912, the Oats King in 1915, and now the Wheat King in 1916.

What was the secret of this man's cropping successes? He answered obliquely, with a plea: "Take your soil seriously! Every soil has a potential far above what most of us discover in it."

10
FOOD WILL WIN THE WAR

War, weather, and wheat were the leading topics of conversation as farmers and townsmen met on the new plank sidewalks fronting Nobleford's foremost structures, the Merchant's Bank, the Noble Foundation General Store, the Foundation's new McDougall House Hotel, and what was popularly known as "Charlie Noble's United Church," affiliated with the Presbyterian Church of Canada. The last, officially opened on March 10, 1918, was "Charlie Noble's Church" because he was the chairman of the building committee and the board of managers, an elder, and one whose attendance at services was as unfailing as the coming of Sunday.

The passing of the politically charged Canadian Conscription Bill in August, 1917, brought out the intensity of the war feeling. After three long years of conflict on a scale such as the world had never known, there was still no clear indication of the outcome. The entry of the United States in April, 1917, brought fresh muscle to the side of the Allies but Britishers, having used up much of their resources, knew they were fighting with "backs to the wall." Casualties were high and the food situation was more critical. German submarines, in their vicious attacks upon Atlantic shipping, failed to force British surrender but were a continuing threat.

All thoughtful people found reason to be worried, and Mr. and Mrs. Noble, avidly following the day-to-day news from the war front, were among southern Alberta's most concerned and patriotic citizens. Nobody was more faithful and generous in support of causes like the Red Cross. The Nobleford Branch of the Red Cross, with Rev. W. C. Marsh as chairman and Mrs. Noble as vice chairman, was said to be the most active in the area. And as president of the first local of the Women's Institute, Mrs. Noble was seeing to it that this organization was doing its full share of war work. When there was to be a bazaar or lawn social in support of the Red Cross, it was a foregone conclusion that it would be at the Noble home.

When the local branch of the Red Cross held a Tag Day in October, 1917, the receipts totalled $681.55, of which $500 was a single contribution from Mr. and Mrs. Noble.[1] And in the next year when citizens were asked to donate articles for an auction sale from which all proceeds would go to the Red Cross, Mrs. Noble gave a parlor table and Charlie gave a building lot in the village, a two-furrow gang plow, and a set of drag harrows, valued altogether at over $700.[2]

The Nobles, of course, were like that in every worthy community cause, in either peace or war, but Charlie had declared, in keeping with the wartime call to all adults not in the armed services, to work harder than ever. The big farm would have taxed another man to the limit of his capacity, leaving no time for other activities. It was not that Charlie had any desire to be active in politics — like his friend and former neighbor Louise McKinney, who by her election to the Alberta Legislature in June, 1917, won the distinction of being the first woman to occupy a legislative seat in the British Empire — but if the Nobleford neighbors wanted him to be a trustee and chairman of the school board, he was ready to serve and did serve. If they wanted him to be the first reeve of the village following incorporation on March 2, 1918, he would find the time — and did. He was returned for a second term and then a third, and it was only after sitting with elected councillors F. W. Hunt and William Harris and the appointed village secretary-treasurer, E. C. Cranstoun, that the public learned that the reeve not only was making a special wartime sacrifice in order to fill the position, but also was providing space for the village administration and personally paying the secretary's salary.[3]

As reeve, Noble did not let the village people forget their wartime obligations. Loafers and shirkers were reminded of their failures, and everybody heard that waste of food and less than full production when human hunger was widespread were outright sins. The rate at which cargoes of wheat and other essential products were being sent to the floor of the ocean was bound to hasten the suffering created by shortages and the necessity of food rationing. It was a serious matter. Nobody knew where it would end. Germany's Vice Admiral Capelle was bragging early in 1918 that submarine warfare and starvation would still be the means of winning the war for his side. British reports of submarine destruction, he said, were exaggerated. His subs were sinking ocean-going ships from three to six times as fast as the British shipyards could replace them, while his underwater destroyers were being built and launched faster than they were being knocked out by the newest antisubmarine inventions.

By 1917 the hint of famine was reaching Canadian dining tables, and in the next year, food rationing had arrived. National Food Board regulations, given the force of law by Order-in-Council, led to the disappearance of sugar bowls and butter bowls from the tables of restaurants and hotels, and customers had to accept rationed helpings of not more than three lumps of sugar and one pat of butter per person, per meal. Wheat bread and meats were being curtailed. Beef and veal could not be served on two named days each week and were restricted to one meal on each other day. Pork was in a similar position, and authorities hoped the same restrictions would be applied voluntarily in the country's homes. About the only fleshy food on the unrestricted list was fish. But Canadians did not know the worst of rationing; the people of France were living with three meatless days each week, and those of Italy, four days per week.

United States had rationing too, and one who felt the crunch mentioned "the wheatless Mondays and Wednesdays, meatless Tuesdays, porkless Sundays, gasless Sundays," and with saloons closed two days a week, there were "boozeless Sundays and Mondays."

"Food will win the war" was the message blazoned across the farming country. The planting acreage was about sixteen per cent higher in 1917 than in 1916, but men on the land were being told to plant still more in 1918 and to raise more cattle and pigs and poultry. Hopefully, the increase in animal products would be accomplished with little or none of the grains that might be used for human consumption. Beef producers were to utilize more wild vegetation, and pig raisers were urged to convert more green crops and hotel and restaurant garbage to pork.

The CPR joined in the "chorus," combining a patriotic message with a "pitch" to sell land: "Food will win the war. Serve your country and yourself by raising food on the fertile plains of Western Canada. The Canadian Pacific Railway makes it easy for you to begin. Lands $11.00 to $30.00 an acre; irrigated lands up to $50; 20 years to pay."[4]

There should not be an idle man or an idle acre in Canada, Hon. T. A. Crerar was saying. "Despite the difficulties, we must produce more food than we have ever done before.... Plan to bring as much new land under cultivation for another crop as possible."[5] To this, the popular Hon. Charles Dunning, speaking as a member of the Dominion Food Board, added that if there was not enough farm help for such an enlarged program, an approach would have to be made to the towns and cities to enlist women and high school students. Every reasonable means should be employed to break more land in 1918.

Charles Noble had the feeling that Crerar and Dunning were talking to him.

Moreover, wartime prices had risen to make food production profitable as well as patriotic. No. 1 Northern wheat, trading at Winnipeg at 84½ cents a bushel at the beginning of the war, reached two dollars a bushel by November 9, 1916. It was a case of prices reacting to scarcity and anticipated scarcity. Any surplus of wheat in Russia was effectively locked up by the war. Argentina had no surplus, and Australian wheat was too far away in the light of shipping difficulties. When wheat prices continued to soar, the Canadian government moved to impose controls and appointed a Board of Grain Supervisors consisting of eleven members — about half of them from the Winnipeg Grain Exchange. The board members were announced on June 11, 1917, and the first action consisted of fixing a maximum price of $2.40 per bushel on No. 1 Northern wheat at Fort William, this to be effective at the first of August following. Farmers had mixed feelings about a ceiling price on wheat when they had lived so long without a floor price.

Nevertheless, after two big crops in 1915 and 1916, many farming people were enjoying a taste of prosperity. Some were buying new cars. Charlie Noble brought home a new Franklin, the finest on the Nobleford roads. Others were buying Fordson tractors being distributed as Canada's Greater Production Fleet at $795 delivered at points of purchase. Still others were investing in more land, and a few were treating themselves to a winter holiday, their first. When a special California-bound train left Lethbridge at 3:15 a.m. on January 5, 1917, most of the tourists were southern Alberta grain farmers, hoping to leave their farming cares behind them for a spell.

This brush with prosperity that resulted in an increased trade in farm lands found Charlie Noble as both a buyer and a seller. It was in his blood to be dealing in farm lands. Some people had an instinctive urge to be trading horses or mules, and some could not stay away from gambling in speculative stocks. With Noble the trading obsession was clearly land, and generally, he bought more than he sold and his holdings continued to grow. He bought two more places in 1916, the James Nelson farm of 1,440 acres at Barons, paying forty-one dollars per acre for it, and about a month later, the Crescent farm or ranch west of Calgary, another three sections.

But neither of these was likely to change the country's output of grain more than slightly; neither presented the opportunity or challenge of unbroken wheat land of which W. J. Stevens of the Alberta Department of Agriculture was talking when he addressed the Western Stock Growers' Association at Fort Macleod in 1916. The province, Stevens declared, had too many acres of useful land producing nothing but ungrazed grass. For a country fighting famine, it was an out-and-out extravagance, and Charlie Noble agreed. The same conclusion had come to him earlier when he saw or thought about the big and excellent and slightly isolated tract of land known as the Cameron Ranch, some thirty miles east of Nobleford.

He did not need any more land, and in buying more, he seemed to be contradicting his own advice given from the public platform. Most people should farm less and farm it better. But nobody could say that he was not farming well. In 1916 he was described as the "best tiller of the soil in southern Alberta," and he couldn't be expected to do better than that, regardless of the size of his operations. He seemed to be rationalizing and compulsively reaching out for more land at the same time.

Anyway, the big Cameron spread had been casting a sort of hypnotic spell over him ever since he had seen it a few years earlier. Now, if it was really a farmer's wartime duty to extend his cultivated acreage, he was ready to tackle something as big as the "Cameron," hoping that it would be profitable as well as patriotic.

Noble paused to study this thing called the "Cameron" and discovered that the ranch's history was about as rich as its soil and was peppered with names of empire builders, names like Roderick William Cameron, ultimately Sir Roderick, from whom the ranch took its name. For students of western Canadian history, Roderick's father, Duncan Cameron of the North West Company, was the wintering partner in charge of Fort Gibraltar at the mouth of the Assiniboine River until arrested by Colin Robertson on charges growing out of the conflict between the men of the fur trade and the Selkirk Settlement. As Colin Robertson's prisoner, Duncan Cameron was being taken to England to face trial and thereby missed the Battle of Seven Oaks in 1816, a triumph for Cuthbert Grant's Métis, a tragedy for the settlement.

In England, Cameron was acquitted of the charges brought against him, and he then claimed and won legal damages on account of his arrest and loss of freedom. On returning to North America, he settled in Glengarry and represented his area in the legislature of Upper Canada from 1820 to 1824. There, in Glengarry, his son Roderick was born on July 25, 1825.

Going as a young man to New York, Roderick Cameron became a most successful businessman and financier. His company, R. W. Cameron and Co., operated ships sailing between New York and Australia, and Cameron served as Canada's commissioner at the Australian international exhibitions in Sydney and Melbourne in 1880. Three years later, he was knighted. By this time he was a man of great financial means and great influence. One of his hobbies was in breeding Thoroughbred horses on his Clifton Stud Farm on Staten Island. His stallion, Leamington, proved to be one of the greatest Thoroughbreds of his time.

In 1889, Cameron began buying western lands, presumably with the intention of cattle ranching. O. S. Longman, in his studies concerning the ranch, concluded that Sir Roderick bought outright some 30,626 acres from the Alberta Railway and Coal Company, paying one dollar per acre for most of it. The land transfers were signed by E. G. Galt, attorney for the railway company. This was, no doubt, crown land granted to the Alberta Railway and Coal Company in payment for building 174 miles of railroad in what is now southern Alberta, at a time when rail construction could qualify for land grants at the rate of 6,400 acres per mile. It is recorded that the railway builders received a land grant totalling 1,114,368 acres.[6]

Sir Roderick died in 1900 without ever making more than slight use of his grassland. He did place a band of Shetland ponies on the place with the thought of producing pit ponies for use in the Belly River coal mines in which he was interested. Dr. T. Childs, who worked for many years in the service of the Health of Animals Branch in western Canada, moved with his parents to live beside the river in 1902 and recalled "several hundred Shetland ponies" running on the Cameron place but had nothing to offer about the ponies as beasts of burden.[7]

Some ponies may have gone to the mines, but story had it that the range band suffered and ultimately disappeared as a result of attacks by wolves.[8]

Anyway, there it was, as Noble saw it, almost all of township 11, range 18, west of the fourth meridian, something over 20,000 acres. The rumor reached Noble's ears in October, 1916, that the owners were interested in selling the entire tract, either in one piece or divided into small farms. As soon as seeding was completed the next spring, Charles with eleven-year-old son Shirley drove over the property. As the latter remembered the trip across what looked like a shoreless sea of grass, "several small herds of antelope ran from us and a fat coyote slunk away through the tall grass, but there were very few cattle on it at the time. It looked too good to resist and dad drove directly to Lethbridge."[9]

There may have been an additional reason for hurry: As Charlie Noble admitted later, he saw strangers on the land, obviously studying its worth. He had a hunch that these were prospective buyers and the hunch was correct. The visitors were from New York and considering purchase.

Driving directly to the law office of the firm of Connebeare, Church, and McArthur, agent for the Cameron estate, Mr. Noble submitted an offer of fifteen dollars an acre for his choice of eight sections and with it a deposit of $5,000. At the same time, he was taking an option on the balance of the land in the township. With only little delay, the offer was accepted, and roughly 20,000 acres were added to the Noble Foundation farms, bringing the total land inventory to almost 33,000 acres in seven farm units.

It took much nerve and courage, especially in a dry year. But Noble had both, and when one hundred urbanites from Lethbridge accepted his annual invitation to visit the farm at harvest time in that year of 1917, they saw 10,000 acres of crop that seemed to contradict the dry summer. It was his biggest seeded acreage to date because, in response to the public pleading for greater production, he departed from his practice of summerfallowing close to half of his land and planted considerable crop on spring-plowed land.

The big fields could this year show 3,582 acres of wheat on summerfallow, 3,660 acres of wheat on spring plowing, 1,570 acres of oats on spring plowing, 500 acres of rye on summerfallow, 235 acres of flax on spring plowing, 150 acres of corn, and 40 acres of potatoes, making a total of 9,777 acres actually under crop. The wheat on summerfallow seemed to promise forty-five bushels per acre, and the wheat on stubble ground, about half as much. The visitors from the city were much impressed by operations, as they should have been, and no less impressed by the organization and costs on such a farm — 40 binders in use simultaneously; 250 horses and mules eating $125 worth of feed every day; 150 hired men receiving wages averaging $4 per day; and total operating costs of $1,200 per day.[10]

So large was the operation of grain growing that a herd of 400 cattle was too often overlooked. The annual stock-reducing auction sale gave proof of the mixed farming character of the Noble business. The surplus stock being offered by auction in one of those years consisted of 40 horses, 1 breeding jack, 40 cattle, 1 purebred Holstein bull, 25 bred sows, 150 chickens, and 10 purebred Shorthorn bulls contributed to the sale by the Honorable Duncan Marshall. Also included in the items about to be offered was a quantity of 20,000 bushels of Noble's seed oats, all ready for the drill. It should have been enough to remove all doubt concerning the mixed farming character of the Noble enterprise.

Charlie's older brother Newell James Noble, who had been a source of help and encouragement for six years, was sorry to be leaving Nobleford at this exciting moment in local history when the big farm was being doubled in size, when the new Charles Noble home was nearing completion to be seen as one of the finest in southern Alberta, and when the progressive profit-sharing features of the Foundation to which he had brought professional legal guidance were being put to the practical test. Now "N.J." and his wife were returning to the United States, and the home they had occupied was being taken over by Ernie Rubie, who had come very recently from Calgary to manage the grocery department of the Noble Foundation General Store which was under the general management of William Buchanan. Rubie, who was to become a prominent figure, had reason to be pleased with the Nobleford welcome, except for Nature's part consisting of a violent June storm that left the store with a gapping hole in one wall and the local correspondent for the *Lethbridge Herald* with an original idea of what happened. "When the storm was at its height," according to the report, "a thunderbolt fell and burst on the northeast corner of the building occupied by the Noble Foundation General Store."[11]

Unfortunately, there were still bigger "thunderbolts" to fall. Not only was 1917 a dry year with total precipitation of only 12.03 inches at Lethbridge, but also as time was to demonstrate, it marked the onset of a six-year dry period, hard enough on ordinary farm operations in the prairie region and especially difficult for big farms with correspondingly high costs and high debts.

The Cameron land afforded no harvest except native hay in 1917, but having bought the almost overpowering expanse of property, Noble began at once to prepare it for production. There were roads to make, fences to construct, land to break, wells to drill, and houses and barns and sheds to erect, all on a costly scale. While forty binders were at work on the developed crop land, well drillers and fence-building crews were moving upon the Cameron, and wagon trains loaded with building materials were being hauled over the prairies by one of the mighty steam tractors. A picture was printed showing the steamer pulling twelve wagons loaded with 48,000 feet of lumber, on its way to what was to become the biggest single-unit grain farm in the British Empire.

If, as intended, most of the Cameron land were to be broken and cultivated in 1918, it would be important to bring order and organization to the work and to minimize the cost of travelling back and forth. The land to be broken would be divided into four working units — stations A, B, C, and D — each with a farm headquarters presided over by a farm foreman. One of these would serve, also, as the general headquarters where the work on the entire Cameron would be coordinated.

As soon as the arrival of spring was confirmed in 1918, a crew of Noble's workmen and one of the powerful Reeves steamers were making a graded road where previously there had been only a thirty-mile track in the grass, linking Nobleford and the Cameron. Hitched to the steamer were two Adams road graders, and with a crew of seven men, the road was built at a rate of two miles per day and a cost of fifty dollars per mile. Neighbors along the route were glad to be getting a graded road at no cost to themselves.[12]

Buildings were being erected simultaneously at all four headquarter locations. Each site was getting a bungalow for the foreman, a big dormitory with recreation room and dining hall for workmen, a 150-foot long barn to accommodate one hundred horses or mules, and a machine shed and garage. Every site would have a water well and an auxiliary supply of water trapped behind dams in nearby coulees. There would be an electric lighting plant at every location, and all the sites would be connected with private telephones.

Nothing like it had been seen in prairie farming, and an

editor observed that Mr. Noble was spending a fortune and risking a fortune.

Then, at about the first of June when plowing of the virgin prairie began, visitors witnessed the most spectacular display of power farming that the West had produced. Ten Herculean steamer traction engines — most of them carrying the Reeves trademark — and two heavy, single-cylinder, gasoline-powered tractors went into the fields simultaneously. Each of the steam engines pulled a ten-furrow breaking gang and a packer, and each gasoline engine pulled eight bottoms and packer. It made for a total of 116 breaking plows turning sod, and with engineers and all members of the big crew working in shifts, the tractors and plows were in motion as long as there was daylight, turning over about 400 acres of sodland every twenty-four hours, every day except Sunday because nobody on Charlie Noble's farm did more than the essential work on that day.

For the engineers and other members of the breaking crews there were medals and cash bonus payments payable to the men who could show the biggest areas of breaking during the season. And when the time for good breaking ended in late June, almost 16,000 acres of the Cameron land had been plowed and some of it was already seeded.

Mr. Noble was well aware that seeding on new ground almost right away was not regarded as good practice. It was better to allow the grass and root masses to rot and let the land lie fallow for the remainder of the first year, but under the stress of war, there was an urgency about getting crops, even small ones, and many rules were changed. Mr. Noble planted about one third of the 16,000 freshly broken acres to flax, one third to oats, and marked the remaining one third to receive the conventional fallow treatment that would be conducive to the best crop in the next year.

On the older land owned by the Noble Foundation in 1918, crop yields reflected the dry summer season but came through well enough to bring surprise to visitors and neighbors. The average yield of wheat, according to the annual report, was twenty-four bushels to the acre, and of oats, fifty bushels. In the light of the droughty circumstances, there was every reason to be pleased with such returns, but at the Cameron ranch where so much of the year's work was performed, there was no reason to cheer. As a result of the dry summer and hasty seeding, the flax was close to a failure; only 4,000 bushels were recovered from 5,000 acres. It meant, of course, that most of the flax acreage was not cut at all. The oats on the new breaking gave only a crop of greenfeed. It would be costly feed for the horses and mules.

For the Noble Foundation with its huge investment in agriculture and relatively small involvement in the store and hotel and other enterprises, the net profit on the 1918 operations was $34,666, not very much when the overhead was considered. Nevertheless, by drawing moderately from the company's reserves, the year's dividend payable to shareholders was set at fifteen per cent, down considerably from the twenty-five per cent declared in the previous year.

The president took the opportunity to say through the annual report that "the profit-sharing scheme has been a wonderful success. . . . Many employees have invested in the company and are now drawing dividends on paid up stock."[13]

War ended with the signing of the Armistice on November 11, and Canadians, while engaged in another war against an epidemic of Spanish influenza, rejoiced at the prospect of peace. They knew that the formal end to hostilities would not solve all their problems, but they were hopeful, and members of the new board of directors of Noble Foundation, Limited — C. S. Noble, E. C. Cranstoun, W. J. Buchanan, Max Englebretson, E. J. Rossiter, W. J. Dalgliesh, and F. W. Kienbaum — were optimistic. Charles Noble, still the "Chief" and for all practical purposes the owner of the oversized farming enterprise, could find reason for both comfort and sleepless nights in the knowledge that his assets totalled about two million dollars and his debts over half a million.

Charles Noble with his father, H. E. Noble, and brothers. From left to right: Will, H. E. Noble, Guy, Charles, Earl, and Lloyd (partially obscured), c. 1900.

The Charles Noble family residence in Claresholm, 1907. The house was later used as the town hospital.

*Charles and Margaret Noble
with their daughter, Alleen
and sons Gerald and Shirley
(standing), c. 1915.*

*A measured field of exactly 100 acres yielded 130 bushels of oats per
acre in 1915. A 1000-acre field on the Noble farm in the same year
averaged 126 bushels per acre — another record.*

The Lethbridge Board of Trade members visiting the Noble farm to see the world record wheat crop of 1916.

Harvesting the record wheat crop of 1916.

Eleven Reeves steam tractors and one Case, each pulling twelve-furrow breaking gangs, were used twenty-four hours a day to break most of the Cameron Ranch in 1917.

Plowing with ten-horse units at the Cameron Ranch, c. 1918. Horses were used after the initial breaking with steam power.

Hauling water in wooden tanks to service steam tractors and working horses in 1918. The five tanks hitched together held 140 barrels of water.

A sixteen-mule team pulling drills for seeding in 1918. One of the big farm units on the Cameron Ranch was stocked exclusively with "mule power."

The cable car over the Old Man River, north of Chin, Alberta. It was built to shorten the hauling distance for grain from the Noble fields to market.

Eight cultivating units, each consisting of ten horses and one teamster, at the Cameron Ranch, c. 1920.

The Mountain View Farm, one of the Noble Foundation units.

The Noble Foundation store at Nobleford, c. 1920.

Hitching for a day in the fields on the Cameron Ranch main farm, c. 1920. The site of the big barn is now part of the Cameron Hutterite Colony.

Charles Noble, left foreground, at work at the Grand View farm, c. 1928.

Seeding with three Van Brunt drills drawn by a crawler-type tractor, c. 1932.

One of the first three Noble Blades built in 1936. It was restored for the sixtieth anniversary of Nobleford in 1969.

The village of Nobleford and the original Noble factory in 1949. The pile of white doors in the open field at the left are the wall sections of the present factory. C. S. Noble purchased them from a nearby air training field as war surplus.

Charles Noble with the spade, turning the first sod for the new Noble factory at Nobleford in 1950.

The 1950 models of the Noble Blade.

Charles Noble, taken on the occasion of the grand opening of the present factory in 1951.

11
POSTWAR WORRIES

War's end brought rejoicing, but as Canadians were soon to discover, the postwar years held dire problems too. Herbert Hoover, who was destined to become the thirty-first president of the United States, was appointed director general of the International Food Commission and, going at once to Europe, reported that massive amounts of food supplies were needed quickly if starvation and anarchy were to be prevented.

For prairie farmers, the most grievous problems were falling prices for agricultural products, recurring drought, and drifting soil. Government haste in terminating all wartime measures, including the Board of Grain Supervisors and the fixed prices initiated by the board, brought rural unrest. Farmers who had been showered with government attention during the war now seemed to be the forgotten people. Rather grudgingly, a Canadian Wheat Board was constituted to market the crop of 1919 and then withdrawn, allowing grain sales to revert to the open market on which farmers seemed to be repeatedly selling grain at "the wrong time."

Charlie Noble was constantly taking his chances with crops and weather, but he was not a gambler in the ordinary sense of the term. Nor was he a complainer, but with his heavy investment and debt, nobody on the land had more about which to worry.

Farmers generally reacted with a new interest in direct political involvement. Ontario, late in 1919, elected a Farmers' Government, and two years later, Alberta did the same, sending thirty-nine United Farmers of Alberta candidates to sit as members in the legislature. Then, later in the same year, 1921, sixty-five farmer candidates were elected to sit as Progressives in the House of Commons, under the leadership of T. A. Crerar of Manitoba. Farmers gave the impression of being "on the march," although not all in step.

Charlie Noble, by this time widely known, came in for some criticism because he did not appear at the forefront in this so-called agrarian revolt. No doubt his influence would have been useful in the farmers' movement at that time, but his nature explained his absence. He was never one of the militants, and in his contact with people, he was retiring more than aggressive. The family background in the United States was Republican, but as a Canadian he leaned toward the Liberal Party. He was, however, quite willing to leave active party politics to others. As the slightly bashful individualist, he wanted to be a good citizen by being a good neighbor, a good churchman, and a good farmer.

Unchanging was the moral fervor in his desire to give his soil the kind of watchful care a mother would have for her infant, and if he could fulfill the high hope on a big-farm scale, the triumph would be even more satisfying.

Unfortunately, however, no amount of loving care directed at soil would bring rain when it was needed or insure satisfactory prices to match the rising costs in production and capital debts incurred during the war. The six years 1911 to 1916, inclusive, showed an average precipitation at Lethbridge of 17.84 inches and were fruitful and moderately profitable for farmers, but the next six, 1917 to 1922, were lean years, averaging only 11.85 inches. Noble's crops on summerfallow were generally good, even in isolated dry years, but a succession of dry years could and did curtail moisture reserves in summerfallow soil, and 1919 was an almost total failure, reflecting the extremely limited rainfall and snowfall in the previous year.

The Little Bow River went dry in late 1918 and remained so throughout much of 1919.[1] Clouds of drifting soil appeared with menacing frequency and community life was depressed. The nearby village of Barons was taking the drought so seriously that its citizens' committee cancelled all plans for the summer Chautauqua program. Also in keeping with the threat of drought-induced hard times, residents of the nearby Keho School District, when planning a community social, declared it to be a "Gopher Festival." The prairie gophers, correctly called Richardson ground squirrels, had always seemed more ravenous and destructive in dry years, and to aid in control of the rodents, Keho residents were invited to the evening of entertainment with admission payable in gopher tails. The proceeds from the evening totalled 7,101 gopher tails.

By late July, the *Manitoba Free Press* declared the western crop to be the poorest in many years, and prairie farmers were again asking for an extension of the benefits of irrigation and enquiring hopefully about the alleged wonders performed by a California "rainmaker," Charles Mallory Hatfield. His mysterious services were being sought at many points extending from Mexico to the Yukon, and he made the most of his opportunities in gaining publicity while divulging as little as possible about the technicalities of his operations, beyond talking about his "chemicals" placed in broad evaporating tanks on top of thirty-five-foot towers erected at the sites of prescribed areas.

Farmers in several western Canadian districts — at least two of them near Nobleford — opened discussions and then negotiations with Hatfield. A Vulcan Alberta spokesman tried to get the rainmaker's interest but received no reply to his letter. In the case of the dry land farmers at Burdett, a deal was all but signed when Hatfield came in for some harsh criticism on his home ground. An American meteorologist with the United States Department of Agriculture said: "We are not ignorant of the forces that produce rain," then referred to Hatfield's methods as "absurd."[2] Coincidentally, the Burdett district received a heavy rain about the time this unfavorable comment was being repeated, and it took nothing more than an argument about a "No rain, No pay" clause in the contract to cause a breakdown in relations between Burdett and Hatfield. All that survived was a limerick and not a very good one:

There was a young man from Burdett,
Who wanted to get his skin wet
By the rainmaker's art.
But the clouds fell apart,
So he sticks to his money, you bet.

But the Canadian West would hear more of Hatfield, mainly in connection with the fulfillment of a contract at Medicine Hat in the next year.

One of the side effects of the dry year of 1919 was the significant increase in soil drifting. Charles Noble's land was not one of the first to drift, but he was certainly one of the first to talk in alarming terms about the dangers. Although his practice of summerfallowing extensively might have been expected to hasten soil erosion, his early pursuit of a lumpy surface no doubt delayed the menace. Now it appeared that the lumpy surface was no longer adequate, and a press report in June told that "soil drifting in the Nobleford district is engaging the serious attention of farmers and it is understood a convention is to be held shortly to discuss ways and means of putting a stop to the menace."[3]

The experience of that spring was enough to win Noble's unending support for the mounting battle against soil erosion. His new determination to fight the forces causing drifting to the finish may have been the best farm return of the year.

Many crops planted on stubble around Nobleford and Barons in that first postwar year were complete failures, and it had to be seen as a further tribute to Noble's meticulous summerfallowing methods that the Foundation could report average yields of even eight bushels of wheat and ten bushels of oats per acre.

With high operating costs and large interest payments to be met, it was an unprofitable year for the Noble Foundation. Even before the severity of the drought was known, Mr. Noble visited the United States and sold a quarter-million-dollar bond issue. The *Alberta Gazette*, over the name of the registrar of joint stock companies, announced that the capital stock of the Noble Foundation, Limited, "is this day [June 6, 1919] increased from $750,000 to $1,000,000 by the creation of 2,500 new shares of the par value of $100 each."[4]

The new money was needed and the increased obligation could have been carried without difficulty in a year of a rewarding harvest, but as the crop season turned out, the Foundation's financial position deteriorated too much for a proprietor's peace of mind. Noble, by the end of 1919, might have regretted the earlier decision to buy the Cameron Ranch which had not yet given even a moderate return. But if he had any regrets, he did not say so. He was not one to parade his worries.

But "next year" would be better. It was the spirit that kept many dry country farmers from going mad. Noble was not a pessimist and he was not an irresponsible optimist. He wanted to be a realist and knew that by the law of averages, the next year should be better. And so it was; 1920 was much better. It, too, was a relatively dry year, but Noble was better prepared for it and succeeded in recovering enough grain to qualify for an unsought international distinction. In terms of grain production alone, 1920 was the biggest year in Charles Noble's career, and he was proclaimed the largest producer of grain in the British Empire.

The early season reports from the farm told of an unusually wet spring and announced the planting program for 19,600 acres of cultivated ground. Intended plantings included 11,980 acres of wheat, 2,960 acres of oats, 3,740 acres of rye, and 920 acres of flax. The report added that: "About 250 teams will be used in putting in the crop and the cost of [seeding] operations will be somewhere in the neighborhood of a quarter of a million dollars."[5]

Two days later, readers were informed about a one-day seeding record made by the Foundation's drills, 1,200 acres of land seeded in a single day by twenty-six four-horse seed drills working in two shifts of nine hours each.[6] This was not a publicity stunt but rather an average day in the planting program. The same rate of seeding, it was expected, would continue until all the seed was in the ground, thereby taking fifteen days to cover 19,600 acres.

Before the spring-seeded crops were advanced sufficiently to protect the soil's surface from the spring winds, southern Alberta was experiencing dust storms that made farmers say, "The worst yet." The particular day they were to remember was June 8, when most bare fields suffered and clouds of silt cut off the rays of the sun, making noonday seem like an evening hour. Children were known to become temporarily lost when returning from school.

It wreaked damage to exposed fields, but for farmers searching for cultural methods that would prevent such erosion, it proved to be a useful demonstration. Anybody who was continuing to practise the long-popular dust mulch type of summerfallow was in serious trouble and saw tons of soil leaving his fields. Charlie Noble's lumpy surface came through moderately well, but not well enough to suit him.

The Koole Brothers — Arie and Leonard — immigrants from Holland farming at nearby Monarch, found reassurance in the strip farming technique they had adopted. Their alternating strips of summerfallow and seeded crop, each ten rods wide and running at right angles to the direction of the prevailing wind, came through with a minimum of damage and were soon attracting enquiring visitors from far and near.

The severe dust storm of that early June day proved to be an effective awakening. Farm conferences were called for discussions of the soil problems. The first one was held in Charlie Noble's office at Nobleford about two weeks after the big blow, expressly to consider the new and growing threats of soil drifting and cutworm depredations. The entomologist from the Lethbridge Experimental Station was present to answer questions about cutworms, while Superintendent William H. Fairfield of the same station, and James Murray and Charles Noble of the Foundation, talked about the mounting fears of soil drifting.[7] It marked the beginning of a new campaign to safeguard the great resource of soil.

Hon. C. M. Hamilton, minister of agriculture in Saskatchewan, presided over a conference devoted mainly to soil matters at Swift Current on July 9, and a couple of weeks later, there was an irrigation conference at Lethbridge, at which C. S. Noble was invited to address the gathering on the subject of soil drifting. When he was unable to be present, his able assistant James Murray, the man who had been superintendent of the Brandon Experimental Farm and joined the Noble Foundation as superintendent of the farms, spoke instead and brought the Noble message.

Judging from the experience of the Noble Foundation farms, Murray believed the lumpy surface summerfallow was still the most practical means of control and said that: "Out of 6,000 acres at Nobleford, between 200 and 300 acres had been affected by blowing although the farm was in the area that was so badly damaged on the June 8 of this year."[8]

Noble's zeal to beat the erosion was rising to fever pitch. Not only was he speaking out about soil preservation but also he was writing on the same subject. In a feature article that appeared in the *Lethbridge Herald*, he was pleading for "quick decisions on methods to be adopted and pursued vigorously."[9]

The chief was now convinced of the necessity of advancing the cause of soil conservation through education. Soils and soil preservation should receive more attention in the public schools, he reasoned, and the new interest in school fairs had his approval. When it was announced that the schools of Nobleford and Barons districts would combine to hold one of the sixteen school fairs in southern Alberta in 1920, he gave his support. One of his contributions was a handsome shield for the best school exhibit of sheaf and threshed grains, including wheat, oats, and rye.

Although the day of the fair, September 20, came at the middle of Noble's complex harvesting operations, he took leave of the farm for half a day to encourage the young exhibitors — no doubt his only holiday in the crop season — and presented the big shield to the Nobleford School. There was unrecognized significance in the fact that the fair was the means of Charlie Noble's meeting a kindred soul, O. M. McConkey, who judged the grain and forage classes that day and was later professor of field husbandry at the Ontario Agricultural College and author of a pioneer book on conservation entitled *Conservation In Canada*. The first words in the book would have pleased Noble: "The soil, like freedom, is not appreciated until it is endangered."

Noble would find it difficult to take his thoughts away from harvesting operations in progress that day, but there would be some quiet satisfaction in seeing the children showing a proper interest in the products of the good soil, and especially in noting that his son Shirley won the prize for the best entry of flax and second for rye, while his younger son, Gerald, won the trophy for the best potatoes and second prize for his construction of a plan for a farmstead.[10]

The reporter who left an account said it was one of the biggest and best school fairs but did not mean to leave himself open to suspicion of taking a bribe by accepting the present of a piece of the first prize raisin pie.

Charlie Noble drove away from the fair muttering to himself: "Those kids are the best reasons for putting a stop to the drifting and saving all the goodness in our soils." He was, like Oswald McConkey, making conservation a matter of morals.

12
HISTORIC HARVEST SCENES AT THE CAMERON, 1920

Farm tempo quickened at the harvest season when crop recovery across the West appeared to resemble a mad rush against time and changing weather. It was ever thus. Daylight hours were becoming shorter, and working hours were longer for men, women, and horses. Breakfast was earlier; supper was later; and bedtime for workers with tired muscles was sweeter in those rushed but unforgettable days that began annually with cutting and stooking and ended when the big steam-driven threshing machines gobbled up the last of the sheaves and members of the well organized threshing crews were paid off.

Never were those harvest scenes more dramatic than on the Noble land in that autumn of 1920 when the operations engaged the chief and as many as 160 hired helpers and 300 horses and mules. Never before was one Canadian farming enterprise conducting harvest on as much land, and never had there been an indication of as much threshed grain. And in the light of extensive farm expansion and near crop failure in the previous year, it may be that no debt-ridden farmer had ever experienced greater need for a good crop return.

A reporter visiting the Foundation farms in August thought he saw a "million dollar crop on the Noble fields."[1] He might have been right if it had not been for falling prices. When the short-lived Canadian Wheat Board terminated its dealings and trade was resumed by the Winnipeg Grain Exchange on August 15, 1920, wheat prices strengthened slightly to $2.85 a bushel, basis No. 1 Northern, at Fort William and then began their long and disastrous decline. The country was entering a postwar slump, and before threshing was completed, wheat and other grains were "on the skids."

But threshing came before marketing and Charlie the chief was noticeably more intense. His stride was longer and bolder, and people around him wondered if he was getting any sleep and when he was taking his meals. Only a few understood the burden he was carrying or realized that the task of directing the work force required to harvest a good crop on 20,000 acres of prairie land would probably match that of a field marshal commanding a battlefield campaign.

The year's harvest began with the cutting of roughly six sections of winter rye, that cereal for which Noble was finding greater use and greater respect on account of its soil-saving value. The thick stand and heavy heads reinforced his belief that winter rye was not only a relatively reliable crop but also one of the most useful in furnishing cover and protection for the soil in the spring season when wind erosion was a major threat.

The field of rye that made the chief chuckle was not his best producer but rather one which he did not expect to give him anything. It was a 600-acre area seeded on new breaking two years earlier. In the dry and disappointing year of 1919, it yielded only seven or eight bushels per acre, and it was Noble's intention to plow the stubble and summerfallow the ground in 1920. But to his surprise, the spring brought a fine stand of volunteer rye and plowing was delayed so the area could be used as an early season horse pasture. Then, when the volunteer crop continued to show vigor, Noble decided to give it a chance to mature. The final result was a volunteer crop giving twenty bushels of excellent rye per acre.[2]

Again Mr. Noble invited members of the Lethbridge Board of Trade to visit the farms on a day in August when harvesting was in progress. This time, the Calgary Board of Trade membership received the same invitation, and about 250 visitors from two cities drove to the Cameron Ranch farm on August 18 and saw harvest operations such as they had never witnessed before and would never see again. Those who completed the farm tour could have seen 60 binders, hauled by 240 horses and mules, cutting into the 19,000 acres of crop and might have made their own wild and inconsequential guesses about probable returns in terms of bushels or dollars.

Whatever the exact dollar return, it would be the biggest and most valuable crop to come from one farm anywhere in the British Empire in that year or any previous year.

Overawed visitors learned that the Noble Foundation farm land at that moment totalled 33,090 acres, of which 28,689 acres were under cultivation and the rest was in use for grazing. They might have surmised that since the formation of the Noble and Harris Land Company — a Noble Foundation subsidiary with Charles Noble as president, J. Harris as managing director, and E. C. Cranstoun as secretary — intended to handle purchases and sales, total acreages could fluctuate from day to day like the weather.

There were some unprecedented speeches within the sound of grain binders. The visitors heard Mr. Noble explain his farming ideals and the methods by which he hoped to conserve his soil and bring a complete halt to drifting. He believed that farmers should be keeping more closely in touch with experimental and scientific developments and made a significant plea for what he called "agricultural advisers." These informed individuals would be trained public servants, constantly available to farming people to advise about crop varieties, seeding methods, cultivation, soil management, livestock production, and so on.[3]

His plea was significant because he was again ahead of his time in making a public request for the kind of advisers who were provided ultimately in the agricultural representative services of the provincial departments of agriculture in the West.

The guests were impressed, also, by the remarks made on the same occasion by G. R. Marnoch, president of the Lethbridge Board of Trade, when he pronounced Mr. Noble as one of the best neighbors any rural-urban community could have. His mind is always open to discovery, the president said, and when he has tested something new and found it good, he is anxious to share it with others who can benefit. "A community that has one man of the calibre and experience of W. H. Fairfield, superintendent of the experimental farm here, and another farming on such an extensive and highly efficient scale as C. S. Noble, is very fortunate."[4]

The host of the day was sorry and the visitors were sorry that they were a few days too early to see five steam threshing outfits — two on the Nobleford places and three on the Cameron — starting to work. They were also some days too early to see the recent Noble invention, the cable car, designed to move grain across the Old Man River as a means of shortening the delivery distance to a railroad shipping point. But about the latter they would hear much.

As soon as the winter rye was dry enough and hard enough for threshing, just two days after the sixty binders completed cutting the wheat, the Reeves steamers and the Red River separators moved into threshing positions, and binder operators hitched to bundle wagons and stookers became field pitchers and spike pitchers.

Robert Gratz, who hired with Mr. Noble in 1920 and became a farm foreman, spent most of that harvest season working in the elevator at Chin, which the chief was leasing from the Bawlf Grain Company. In that position, Gratz was taking delivery of 4,000 to 5,000 bushels of Foundation grain every working day and keeping closely in touch with all the threshing operations on the Cameron. As he explained, each threshing outfit was supported by 27 workmen and 54 horses.[5] Thus, the five threshing crews would be employing 135 men. Teamsters were paid $8.00 a day and spike pitchers, $9.60, making a total payroll of at least $1,500 per day. Horses and mules in harness for the threshing numbered about 400.

It was indeed a harvest exercise such as the Canadian countryside had not seen before.

Noble was fair to his men, as most of them were quick to declare, and thoughtful for his horses and mules, but he demanded efficiency and organized to insure it. Each threshing outfit had one engineer, one separator man, one fireman, two tankmen who drove four-horse teams in hauling water for the engine, one "flunky" who used part of his time hauling straw for fuel to the engine, four spike pitchers at the feeder, two men handling the Stewart sheaf loaders, three men with 125-bushel grain tanks and four-horse teams hauling grain from the separator, one or two cooks, and, according to Robert Gratz, up to twelve teamsters with bundle racks hauling from the sheaf loaders to the separator.

When the sheaf loaders were abandoned late in that season, they were replaced by eight field pitchers.

An inventive feature of the Noble threshing methods of that time was the unloading arrangement at the feeder of each separator. Each machine was provided with a big wooden platform at the feeder end on which the bundle racks unloaded automatically with a feeder extension that brought the feeder within a couple of feet of the ground, making it easier for spike pitchers to work from the platform.

To facilitate this feeder-end arrangement, each bundle rack

was provided with a loose or movable gate which rested against the front of the rack until the teamster drove onto the platform, at which time he completed a connection between the gate and a cable anchored to the steam engine. Having fastened the gate or end gate to the engine, he drove away and saw the load of sheaves being dragged off his wagon and deposited on the platform from where the sheaves would be fed into the elongated feeder by the spike pitchers.

Generally, two threshing outfits operated close to each other on the Cameron Ranch farm, enabling the crews of both to share the same movable camp for sleeping and dining. Distances on the Cameron were great, and it would not do for men and horses to be spending a big part of their time moving back and forth on the trails. To remove such an extravagance, movable threshing camps were set up close to the machines. These caboose and tent camps were moved every time the threshing outfits moved, and workmen and horses remained in the fields, close to their work, day and night.

But it was the overhead tramway to carry grain across the river that captured public interest more than any of the other harvest innovations. The long haul from the Cameron place to an elevator that would receive grain — either at Taber or Retlaw — was one of the objections to the property, perhaps one reason why the property had not been developed sooner. When the small amount of grain grown there in the previous year was hauled to an elevator, it had to go twenty-five miles — fifty miles round trip for the teams and teamsters. Again and again Mr. Noble and his men said: "Oh for a bridge across the Old Man River that would allow us to take our grain to Chin on a trail of less than ten miles."

Chin was straight south of the mouth of the Little Bow River, but to reach it from the north side of the Old Man River by way of existing bridges or ferries would entail more trail miles than going to Taber. A shorter haul would be easier on horses, necessitate less granary space on the farm, and make more efficient use of labor. Something had to be done. Mr. Noble vowed that something would be done.

It was the kind of challenge he seemed to enjoy, the way a mountaineer enjoys a climb to the top. He considered building a bridge but cost would make it impractical. He thought of installing his own ferry, but it would not be reliable under the circumstances of changing weather. He caught the idea of storage bins on both sides of the river with cable cars to convey the grain from one side to the other. His decision was to proceed.

As recorded by Mrs. Lillian Noble, daughter-in-law, "Consulting engineers were brought in from Vancouver to advise as to the feasibility of a cable car to carry grain across the river. They advised that it could not be done. Dad said it must be done and so work was started."[6]

First, it was necessary to find a river location with a high and steep bank on the north or farm side and a broad valley with adequate access for wagons on the other or Chin side. Having fixed upon a site, a 50,000-bushel storage bin was built on the steep side and a 5,000-bushel elevated storage bin was built on the south side, about eight miles north of Chin. A cable and cable car or bucket with sixty-bushel capacity was then installed to convey the grain from north side to south side, whence the horse-hauled wagons could be loaded by gravity for the relatively short haul to Chin.

But it was more complex than that. A load of grain from the threshing machines dropped on the north side would fall into the long 50,000-bushel bin constructed on an angle of about thirty-five degrees so grain would slide to the lower end where a mechanical device would release exactly sixty bushels or fifty-five bushels as required into the car or bucket. The loaded carrier would then be propelled across the river on the cable with power from a donkey engine and dumped automatically into the elevated storage on the south side.

It was an $18,000 installation and was ready to use on September 15, 1920. Those who were present to judge its initial performance said it worked perfectly, and every bushel of grain taken across the river was benefiting by a reduction in delivery distance of about fifteen miles.

Noble had an excellent grasp of practical construction principles and chose to supervise the work going into the erection of his own buildings. When the cable car bins were under construction, he personally supervised the making of the long structure resembling a grain elevator lying at a precarious slant on its side, but he could not be on both sides of the river at the same time and left the supervision of the south side building to a foreman.

Whatever the reason — inadequate reinforcing, faulty materials, or excessive wind pressure — trouble overtook the structure on the south side, and at a moment when it was full of grain, its sides collapsed. Nobody was injured, but 5,000 bushels of grain had to be shovelled from the ground into wagons and there was a delay of two or three days while the bin was being repaired and retrussed. But the invention then returned to giving unfailing service, and people drove for miles to see it.

The first grain moved across the river on the cable was a quantity of rye. Robert Gratz said that about eighty carloads of rye were shipped that year, most of it from the Cameron land and most of it through the elevator at Chin where he was working at the time. This grain was brought to Chin by twelve eight-horse teams — each team pulling two grain tanks — and four four-horse teams hauling single grain tanks. Altogether, according to Gratz, they were delivering about 6,000 bushels per day. The teams made two round trips one day and one trip the next to avoid overworking the horses. An auxiliary team or "snatch team" of four horses was kept at the south side bin at all times to provide assistance needed to take the loaded wagons up the hill and out of the river valley.

While the twelve teamsters and over a hundred horses were hauling rye from the river to Chin and getting most of the public attention, there were the members of the other crew hauling from the threshing machines and field bins to the river. Observers like Robert Gratz marvelled at the coordination reflecting the Noble skill. And the famous overhead conveyance constructed at a remote and lonely point on the western countryside to take a ton and a half of grain across the river every three minutes was working well. Apart from the brief delay when the south side bin suffered a break, there were no problems, and Mr. Noble believed that the installation saved so many miles of heavy hauling, it more than paid for itself in a single season.

Members of the board of trade travelling in a party were too early to see the rye and other grains taking the aerial route across the river, but they read in their newspaper on September 16 that the $18,000 apparatus of Charles Noble's creation was in service: "The first trial of the carrier was made yesterday and it worked splendidly."[7] The news brought hundreds of visitors from as far as Medicine Hat, Camrose, and even Great Falls in Montana. And sixty years later when nothing remained except the carefully chosen site with a high and almost forbidding bank on the river's left side, some concrete footings, and a few rusted cast iron gears, visitors were still travelling far out of their way to see where Charlie Noble installed his famous aerial tram to be a link in the transportation of nearly half a million bushels of grain in one year. Although it probably did not even enter his thoughts, he had also built a monument to human resourcefulness.

13
THE POWER STRUGGLE
IN NOBLE'S FIELDS

After starting in 1903 with four undistinguished oxen, farmer Charles Noble came to the immediate postwar years employing the power of ten steam tractors of the biggest kind, two gasoline-driven tractors of similar might, an assortment of small gasoline tractors, a hundred mules, and five hundred draft horses. It probably totalled enough pulling power to drag Calgary's Palliser Hotel off its foundations. And in harnessing and directing such a great fleet of animal and mechanical power units, the task would seem to have been enough to tax the energies of a minister of transportation.

These were, of course, the years that advanced most spectacularly the Canadian agricultural revolution which had scarcely less social and economic impact than the more loudly heralded Industrial Revolution of a few decades earlier. And nowhere was the change from primitive ox power to broncho power to Clydesdale power to steam power and, finally, to the power supplied by internal combustion engines more clearly demonstrated than on the Noble farms.

It was an evolution that matched that of human aids in transportation seen in the same region, beginning with the Indian-fashioned travois and running through ox-drawn Red River carts, horse-drawn covered wagons, buckboards, democrats, buggies, freight wagons, railroads, automobiles, and, finally, aircraft exhibiting every conceivable stage of efficiency and luxury.

The change from animal power to motor power in Canadian agriculture and in Noble's fields came quickly. He adopted the use of a steam tractor for plowing the prairie sod in 1908, one year before his departure from Claresholm and the same year in which the Winnipeg Motor Competition was conducted for the first time. It marked a turning point in the deadly struggle for mastery in furnishing power for the prairie grain fields.

From that time forward, Noble was never without tractor power and he became the biggest user of farm power, but he never lost a strong natural fondness for horses and mules and never really rejected them. Even in later years he confessed they would be his first choice for meeting farm power needs.

By 1916, however, the Noble fields were witnessing a clear three-way contest among horses, steam, and gasoline — a five-way contest if mules and oxen were considered important enough to be candidates. The conflict, not readily resolved, brought heated arguments in every livery stable across the country and debate of more formal kind to most country schools where the most popular Friday night topics were rewordings of country life vs. city life, Clydesdales vs. Percherons, and horse power vs. tractor power.

Noble by this time had used all three — or all five — kinds of power, had used all extensively and was probably in the best position to make comparisons. Moreover, he was anxious, for his own business benefit, to identify the source of the greatest economy and was keeping feed, fuel, and wage records. The question to be answered was not complex: By what kind of power could he plow and cultivate his fields at lowest costs without loss of quality in the work performed? Every farmer in the country wanted the same information or should have wanted the same information, and neither the university experts nor experimental farm workers were providing it.

Each form of power had its staunch supporters although the steam engine's friends were wavering. Gasoline tractor manufacturers and salesmen knew they were pioneering and were motivated by the prospect of big business profits. The horsemen, on the other hand, were driven by both conviction and loyalty. They were the sons and daughters of communities in which all farmers had been horsemen, and most of them very skillful horsemen. They were members of a generation in which every farm boy dreamed of driving the best team of heavy horses on the road or winning the first prize for four-horse teams at the local fair.

To many horsemen, any thought or talk about displacing horses with another form of power was the equivalent of heresy. A representative of a tractor company attending the

International Dry Farming Congress at Lethbridge in 1912 had the nerve to suggest publicly that tractors would soon displace horses for all heavy work on farms and found himself under immediate bombardment from hostile horsemen. He quickly sensed his mistake and left the province promptly.

Canada by 1920 had 3½ million horses — most of them in the three midwestern provinces. The average farmer in these parts, with ten sets of harness and collars hanging in his stable, pumped water and carried feed for that number of horses — and wished he had a few more. The commonplace appearance of Clydesdale, Percheron, and Belgian stallions "travelling" on country roads and the size of breeding classes at fairs and exhibitions — like the twenty-eight Clydesdale stallions that lined up to be judged in the aged class alone at Brandon Winter Fair in 1920 — showed clearly how well the draft horse was still entrenched in rural western Canada.

Horsemen might very well see themselves as the guardians of a great tradition and had no intention of surrendering to a costly mechanical monstrosity born in some distant factory. They acted as though they felt secure, but they would still seize an opportunity to heap scorn upon the heads of those individuals who were trying to sell tractor power. Letters sent to the editors of farm papers and magazines showed the loyal horsemen far outnumbering the "rebels" who were admitting an interest in the factory creations. One of the many dedicated horsemen who believed his favorite source of power was an enduring part of Canadian agriculture while the tractor would soon be exposed as a grave error and an impertinence wrote:

> There are people who tell us that the horse is going to be superseded; that the time is coming when he will be unnecessary; a thing of the past so far as farm work is concerned. They also have the foreseeing wisdom which enables them to claim that it is to this lumbering, odorous, laboriously groaning, insentient, mechanical piece of dust-raising deviltry which has already usurped the public highways and left the poor horse in the fence corner ... that we are to look for this astonishing work of evolution. ... No machine will ever take the place of the horse, with its intelligent, quick and easy, agile movements, ever ready and easily adjusted powers, submissive temperament and obedient willingness in all kinds of weather. ...[1]

But neither the horseman's wishful thinking nor the tractor

salesman's prejudiced optimism was enough to settle the great dispute. Farmers wanted something more concrete than an angry horseman's railings; they wanted a simple statement of comparative costs prepared by an unprejudiced authority in whom they could have confidence. The first reports of such kind were those prepared on the Noble Foundation farms, some of them coming directly from Mr. Noble's pen and some from James Murray, who was the company's farm superintendent at the time of the studies.

Charles Noble tried to bury all personal preferences and be entirely fair in conducting this study, but the reports brought encouragement and delight to the horsemen and worry to the promoters of tractors. Horses, the Noble reports showed, were still the best choice for farmers seeking the maximum economy in conducting field work. As seen forty years later, the test results which placed draft horses far ahead of steam tractors, and steam tractors far ahead of gasoline tractors, would seem strange and surprising, but a point not to be overlooked was that while the working potential of a draft horse did not change much in the intervening years, the efficiency of the gasoline tractor was improved dramatically. Also, an important factor in explaining the apparent superiority of the horse in the 1920 studies was Mr. Noble's success in improving field efficiency by the use of horses in larger team units, thereby speeding up the work and reducing the cost of hired labor on an acre basis.

The figures based on discing and harrowing after breaking on the Cameron Ranch were quoted a thousand times in school-house debates, always by the side upholding farm horses in the great power controversy. It was bound to be a telling blow when a debater could quote Charlie Noble's exact words because for people who were familiar with his purposes, his figures were nigh unchallengeable, like Andrew Graham Bell's judgment on telephones or Guglielmo Marconi's on wireless communication.

> In 1918 we had a good opportunity to compare horses, steamers, and gas tractors in working down with discs and harrows several thousand acres of newly broken and rolled land. The gas tractors were of 12 tractive horsepower [12-24 h.p.] and each one pulled three eight-foot discs with harrow behind. The same load was hauled by eight horses driven abreast. Four similar outfits were each handled by a 32 h.p. steam engine. The conditions of weather and soil were unusually favorable and uniform for several months for the various kinds of

power employed. The costs for double discing and harrowing were as follows: horses 42 cents per acre, steamers 60 cents per acre, and gas tractors 70 cents per acre.

In figuring these costs, no depreciation was charged. With this included, the showing would have been much more in favor of the horses as with them the depreciation is very low indeed, whereas with the tractors it is considerable. The conditions of land and weather during the trial were more nearly perfect for tractors than one can reasonably hope for ordinarily, so that we do not think we are overstating it when we say that under average conditions the showing made by tractors in the trial was as good if not better than we might expect for most farm operations.[2]

The gasoline tractors of that time, according to the same Noble testimony, penalized themselves by unreliability. Although only the best men were employed to operate them, delays were frequent, the repair bills were big, and the cost of fuel and oil was high and "becoming higher month by month."

Noble's comment about steamers was somewhat more favorable, especially for the heavy task of breaking. "In breaking prairie we have used steamers extensively and we believe with profit, since we pull heavy rollers behind the plows, pressing down the newly turned sod more effectively than could be done with ordinary packers. . . . In plowing summerfallow we have also used steamers extensively but in this kind of plowing, horses do much better work. The land is kept more nearly level and a more uniform seedbed can be prepared. . . . The delays due to rain are much less frequent with horses than with engines in summerfallow work and our only reason for using them [the tractors] is that we have not yet been able to get our horse power up to the point where all the work can be done in the proper season."

As he expounded further, Noble pointed out that although one big steam tractor with one engineer could do several times as much plowing in a day as an ordinary horse outfit, he could still find no "economy in manpower by using the steamer" because it required four or five other helpers to keep the big thing in motion — a fireman, waterman, at least one man hauling fuel, and one plowman. It meant that one man driving a ten-horse or twelve-horse team could be doing more work per man-hour than was likely to be done by a member of the leviathan steamer crew.

Noble would have been one of the first to admit that changing circumstances caused his cost figures and observations of 1920 to be outdated in a few years. Nevertheless, when the information was prepared and released, it represented an important contribution to western agriculture of the time. At least, nobody had anything better to offer. Most farmers were ready to accept the advice.

In his search for the most economical power and the most efficient way of using hired help, Noble adopted as a sort of standard working unit one teamster and an eight-horse team. Then he believed he could improve upon it, and by selecting his workmen with special care and paying bigger wages where there was proof of experience and skill, he was sending teamsters with three-furrow plows and ten-horse teams to the fields. Finally he was adopting still bigger field units, comprising a proven teamster, twelve horses, and a four-furrow gang plow.

Teams of Paul Bunyan size became the rule in the Noble service. Teamsters hauling grain to the elevator at Chin in the fall of 1920 drove outfits consisting of eight horses per unit, hitched as four pairs in tandem formation, each hauling 250 bushels of rye or wheat in two tank wagons with extended sides. Driving such an outfit on the road and into the elevator was a job for a man with master hands, and the teamsters were proud. Likewise, some of the hauling to the Cameron Ranch during the period of building and development there was done with twelve-horse or twelve-mule teams moving twelve tons of freight piled on gangs of three wagons each. And for hauling water to supply the threshing engines at the Cameron place in 1920, four large water tanks hooked together were hauled by a twelve-horse team driven tandem. Each trip brought 140 barrels of water to the steamers. Some people said it was not practical; Charlie Noble believed it was economical and practical.

Naturally enough, roadway freighting introduced some quite different problems, but after using tractors, trucks, and horses in this area, Noble wrote: "For our freighting we depend largely on horses but during 1918 and 1919 we did a great deal of heavy hauling with two 3½-ton trucks, each hauling four or five tons. Most of the haul was over a graded earth road from 20 to 30 miles. On account of the dry seasons the roads were generally good and few delays were encountered. During the same seasons we did a great deal of freighting with 12-horse teams strung out in pairs, using three or four wagons loaded with from 15 to 20 tons. With the best of care and attention, the trucks required no small amount of repairing and the depreciation was very heavy; with the horse outfits there was less grief and lower bills for both depreciation and repair. We have been forced to conclude that, even under these conditions which look favorable for trucks, our freighting can be done more economically with horses and we have abandoned the trucks, except possibly a light one for errand work."[3]

Keeping constantly in mind the conditions and machines of 1920, it can be noted that Noble was drawing about the same conclusions concerning trucks as he had drawn about gasoline tractors, that there were times and occasions when it was advantageous to have them even though the initial cost was high. "We believe that where they are operated by mechanically inclined owners, better service can be had than where dependence is placed on hired mechanics."

"We believe," he would say in conclusion for that 1920 audience, "that no matter how reasonable engines, parts, and fuel may be, it would be a great mistake to neglect the breeding and working of the best type of farm horses."

It is possible, too, that Mr. Noble's observations as announced in 1920 misled some farming people. A few people wrote to the editors of farm papers to disagree with his conclusions. One correspondent, questioning the merit of Mr. Noble's big horse outfits, said he had found a six-horse team to be enough for one man — whether owner or hired man — to feed and manage and work, and hence the most practical for plowing and other field work.[4] But only Noble backed his theories with figures.

The correspondent had a point, and if any farmer supposed he could use a four-horse team in the field and obtain as much cost advantage over steam and gasoline engines as Noble reported, the farmer would be due for a disappointment. The fact was that Noble created much of the advantage for his horses by using them in bigger team units, thereby effecting savings in manpower costs per acre. There was nothing complex about the tests or the lessons. Moreover, it was every farm operator's privilege to use exactly the same methods of reducing field costs if he chose to press for that result.

Whether other farming people followed his example or not, Noble's adopted policy of hitching bigger horse outfits as a means of reducing labor costs was one of his important contributions to postwar agriculture. The theory was so simple: A man driving eight horses hitched to a three-furrow gang plow or twelve horses hitched to a four-furrow plow would do more of the essential field work and do it more economically than another driving five or six horses and a two-furrow gang.

But putting big horse outfits to work in the fields was not always a simple matter. It called for none but the best men to drive them, and it demanded some special imagination in devising suitable hitches that would be safeguard against side draft and, at the same time, insure that all horses would be working with good footing. It was an unnecessary handicap and positively bad management when horses in a big plowing outfit were hitched in such a way that one or more of them had to suffer the added hardship of having to walk on the soft surface of freshly plowed ground.

For drilling, cultivating, and discing, the horses could be spread out in one row and driven "abreast," but for plowing with four or more horses and a gang plow, it was necessary to adopt the tandem hitch principle or accept high loss of energy — perhaps up to twenty-five per cent — from the extra dead weight imposed by side draft or the equally senseless and cruel practice of forcing certain horses to tramp constantly on soft ground. It was important, therefore, that all multiple-horse outfits plowing in Noble fields or performing roadwork be hitched according to the tandem plan.

An ordinary evener for a two-horse team consisted simply of a piece of strong hardwood or metal with a hole for a draw pin exactly in the center and a clevis hole at each end. But the construction of tandem hitches for big outfits called for ingenuity and careful measurements. Some knowledge of the laws of physics could be of assistance. The Shenandoah tandem plow hitch allowing six or eight or ten horses to work with relative freedom and without loss of good footing became popular after its adoption by Charlie Noble.

It was easy to understand that the driver of an eight-, ten-, or twelve-horse tandem outfit could not be expected to drive with a separate rein to every horse in the team. It was found possible, however, with the aid of a combination of tie chains and "buck straps" to control and drive a big tandem team with only two reins going to the two outside horses in the lead team. In other words, only the lead team was driven by the teamster, and all other horses in the outfit were "tied in" and "bucked back" so the horses largely controlled one another. Tie chains or halter shanks went from bit rings to trace chains or single-trees of horses in the team ahead, and buck straps from bit rings to trace chains of teammates prevented animals from pulling unduly far ahead. Successful operation, of course, would be impossible without very careful adjustment of the ties and chains. But the plan, as publicized widely by the Horse And Mule Association of America, could be made to work well and did work well on the Noble Foundation farms.

Throughout his many years of farming from the homestead to his super farms, Noble never restricted himself to the use of one kind of power, either horses or mechanical, and never would, but he wanted it understood that horses and mules were his choice if he was ever obliged to limit himself. He believed in the high state of economy they were capable of bringing to farming practice and, in addition, he liked them. And as Noble's workmen testified, there were few better horsemen and teamsters than the chief.

Andy Sherman — who grew up in the Nobleford district and began working for Mr. Noble at age of seventeen years in 1935, serving as shop foreman from 1942 to 1979 — said his boss was one of the best horse handlers he ever saw, either with two or four reins. He recalled how the chief loved to steal a few moments of relaxation by seating himself on a triple gang plow, collecting the four reins to take control, then driving away as if burying his cares under the freshly turned furrows. When one of the teamsters was having trouble in keeping a straight course with his twelve-horse team hitched to a gang of three seed drills, Noble took the driver's seat on the elevated platform of his designing and quickly straightened out the horses and the drill marks being imprinted on the field.

And although he would drive himself to long hours and heavy toil, he rebelled at the sight of his horses being overworked or abused in any way. Both his hired men and his horses were well fed. "One of the best things to be said for tractors," he remarked on one occasion, "is the relief from heavy toil and cruel masters they can bring to horses and mules."

14
WHEN THE WALLS CAME TUMBLING DOWN

They were troubled times for Charlie Noble and everybody in agriculture, especially the dry land farmers whose misfortune was compounded by drought accompanying postwar depression.

Troubles, it seemed, travelled in packs, like wolves. Spring rainfall at Lethbridge in 1921 amounted to only one third of the corresponding total in the previous year — 2.15 inches in April and May of 1921 compared with 6.03 inches in 1920. And as the summer advanced, so did the farm problems. The month of June brought hungry hordes of grasshoppers, ready to devour everything "except the barbed wire," and on July 12, a severe hailstorm cut a ragged swath of destruction from Nobleford to the Cameron Ranch farm. According to the first published report of the hail, the 11,500 acres of Noble Foundation crops were "wiped out." The latest injury was not really that bad because crops recovered, but it brought its own moments of anguish, and as if drought, cutworms, hoppers, and hail were not enough to torment the chief, there were falling prices for farm products and a sudden impatience on the part of the Noble creditors.

The fact that other dry land farmers were also in trouble was poor consolation, but they were. Referring to farmers in the neighboring province, the Saskatchewan Grain Growers' Association in its annual report mentioned that: "Their financial position was none too good at the dawn of the year [1921] but at its close it was simply deplorable. No. 1 Northern wheat, F.O.B. Head of the Lakes, was worth $2.04 on January 15, 1921, and on January 5 last, $1.13, a drop of practically 91 cents a bushel, and this was not the lowest point."[1] The same report pointed to the price of prime steers at Winnipeg which had dropped from $9.25 per hundred to $4.50, and the price of the best market pigs from $14.00 to $9.75 per hundred.

During the ensuing months of dry soil and falling market prices, several hundred southern Alberta farmers applied to the provincial government for assistance to move northward with their families, to relocate where crops would be more reliable and people on family farms would find more security. Ironically, some of those making the move were among the hundreds of land seekers who just eleven years earlier had stood for days in long lines at the Dominion Land Office in Lethbridge, waiting for new townships in the big southeastern part of the province to be thrown open for homesteading.

Still, the agriculture of that uneasy year of 1921 was not without highlights of success. For students of agricultural history, one of the high points had to be the beginning of a district agriculturist service in the area, for which Charles Noble might have claimed a measure of credit, as will be explained later, and another significant event was the launching of the soil survey for which, again, the unassuming Noble was one who had been asking and promising support. And still another agricultural triumph was in the success of the Alberta farm politicians when on June 18, no fewer than thirty-nine United Farmers of Alberta candidates were elected to seats in the provincial legislature, leaving only fourteen seats to the Liberals, four to the Independents, and four to Labor. The result was the formation of the first agrarian government in the West.

Although Noble was not a participating political partisan, he approved of the outcome and watched with special interest — and mixed emotions — as his friend and former partner T. C. Milnes won in the Claresholm constituency, defeating another old friend from the homestead year of 1903 Louise McKinney by twenty-seven votes. And while Mrs. McKinney, who was to be remembered as one of Alberta's "Famous Five" women of the time, was defeated, two other members of that illustrious group were elected, namely Nellie McClung, who ran as a Liberal, and Irene Parlby, who ran as a United Farmer and was named to the new provincial cabinet.

Here, indeed, were areas of progress, but nothing could hide the fact that the average prairie farmer was in financial trouble. And Charlie Noble, with a bigger enterprise, was in bigger trouble — too big to benefit from the paltry provincial measures intended to shelter the smaller farm owners from the avaricious debt collectors working for mortgage companies and machinery firms.

Noble was not one to parade his woes or even talk about them, but he had ample reason to worry about an obvious deterioration in his business. After selling $600,000 worth of grain from the crop of 1920, one half of the total returns went at once to his banker. In his words: "$300,000 of the then $590,000 credit was returned to the bank,"[2] while the American bondholders howled their protests about not receiving their share of payment on interest.

But "next year" would be better — Chief Mountain Horse of the Blood Reserve said so — and Noble found himself back at the bank, borrowing money for the 1921 planting of 14,231 acres of crop, 3,545 acres of which would be wheat and 2,837 of rye, while 12,345 acres would be summerfallowed.

The farm's current account was carried by the Merchants Bank, which had opened a branch at Nobleford in 1916 and by 1921, like some of its clients, was experiencing financial difficulties. Moneylenders, generally, had become more hesitant, more fastidious, and more difficult, but in a case like that of the good and honest Charles Noble, the bank felt compelled to advance such further sums as would be needed to plant the crop and thereby protect existing loan investments. But the bank was not the only creditor, and questions arose concerning priorities among the claimants.

As a result of the dispute, the court granted a request for the appointment of a receiver to handle or supervise the affairs of the company, and the press on April 13 carried the news from Calgary that: "By consent of all parties concerned, a receiver has been appointed for the Noble Foundation, Limited, the largest farming corporation in Western Canada, possibly in the world. By a court order issued by Mr. Justice Simmons in Calgary, H. E. McDonald of the inspectorate staff of the Merchants Bank, Calgary, is named as receiver."[3]

Providing background information, the same news story told that: "Several large creditors are interested in the affairs of the Foundation, among them being the Merchants Bank of Canada, the Bankers' Trust, an American institution represented in the present proceedings by A. McLeod Sinclair, K. C. .... Another large creditor is Henry Carstens, Seattle, a private trustee for the debenture holders of the first issue of debentures sold in Seattle by the Noble Foundation. The latter's claim is said to be in the neighborhood of $500,000. . . ." When the Carstens claim was again before the courts two years later, the estimate of indebtedness was "approximately $700,000."

It sounded ominous, whichever figure was accepted, and readers wondered if this was the forerunner of complete collapse of the company. But a further explanation by an officer of the bank placed a slightly different interpretation on the arrangement. The receivership, it was explained, was only a temporary device worked out jointly by the bank, the other creditors, and Mr. Noble for the purpose of conducting the business of the company for the year.

"Large advances in the way of a line of credit were needed from the bank in order to put in the 1921 crop and carry the organization until harvest and the selling of the crop," it was told. Before the bank would consent to advance the large sums needed, it insisted that it be given the first claim on the crop. In order to do this and at the same time satisfy bondholders of the company, arrangements were made that an officer of the bank would act as a temporary receiver. Mr. McDonald, formerly accountant and acting manager of the Merchants Bank here [in Calgary] has been appointed in that capacity. So far as the *Herald* can learn, the assets of the company far exceed the liabilities."[4]

The bank representative could rationalize to his heart's content, but the appointment of the receiver was an unwelcomed and unhappy event for Mr. Noble. He accepted it well enough but it hurt, and there were times when he could not restrain his protests. James Murray, who was Mr. Noble's farm manager at the time, said the presence of the new man of authority "was a sore touch to C. S.," and some "stormy sessions followed. When I left in 1922, the bank was virtually in charge."[5]

While 1921 was beset by more business annoyances and more of the natural forces of crop destruction than usual, Charles Noble was being drawn more and more into public service, and leaders like Hon. Duncan Marshall, minister of agriculture, and W. H. Fairfield, superintendent of the experimental farm at Lethbridge, were seeking and receiving his advice. This man with a religious respect for Nature's gift of soil had urged the minister to get on with a soil survey and then found quiet satisfaction in seeing the important work going forward in the three midwestern provinces in that summer. The first survey crew in Alberta began in the general area of Nanton and Claresholm and worked eastward from there.

Farmers attending the Better Farming Conference at Lethbridge during the year were impressed when he said again that "the day of the big farm has passed." After being introduced to the conference by the chairman, Deputy Minister of Agriculture H. A. Craig, as "the most successful large farmer I have ever known," Mr. Noble proceeded to share the conviction which continued to be difficult for his listeners to understand from him that: "the day of the small farm has arrived." He had never really been a small farmer since homestead days and never would be one, but he could believe in small farms, nevertheless. "The large farms must pass," he added. "They must be cut up into smaller farms and a family placed on [each]. This makes for prosperity and the building of the country."[6]

It was in the course of this speech to the conference that Noble presented the idea of district agriculturists or agricultural representatives as a government service to prairie farmers. Ontario had its "reps" and various American states had the benefit of carefully chosen workers with both practical experience and technical training who were hired by the government and placed in rural communities to advise and help farm families.

The suggestion was received enthusiastically by the conference delegates, and one of the first resolutions passed was an authorization for Mr. Noble and two other delegates to proceed at once to Edmonton and there communicate the request to the provincial government for an immediate program that would make these district agriculturists available. Mr. Noble's presentation made it very clear that the appointed men had to be qualified to interpret the most up-to-date information from experimental farms and universities for the benefit of farmers.

The committee, of which Noble was leader, left for Edmonton the very next day, and what followed seemed to furnish an easy answer to the question raised on a few subsequent occasions: "Who earned the right to be remembered as the father of the idea of district agriculturists in Alberta?"

The press reported that: "Messrs. C. S. Noble, Thos. Judson, and N. D. Mills waited on the government yesterday to press the request for the appointment of agricultural experts . . . to advise and assist the farmers in the district south of Claresholm during the coming season."[7] The Honorable Duncan Marshall, to whom the resolution was first presented, pointed out the great difficulty in securing men who had the requisite training and experience for such work, "but he felt the matter to be so important that he immediately called an assembly of the entire cabinet in order that the deputation might bring the details before the other ministers."

Less than four weeks later, when the minister of agriculture was speaking in the Budget Debate in the legislature, he announced that the district agriculturist program had received the approval of the government and money would be voted as quickly as possible for the implementation of the plan. It was one more important step along the road of agricultural education, and Charles Noble was pleased.

In his presentation to the government and in his report about the presentation, Noble declared more emphatically than ever his faith in the family farm principle. His philosophy came clearly to view as he confessed his dream of the time when large wheat farms would be converted to small farms growing brome grass, rye grass, and sweet clover as well as wheat and rye. There would be poultry and pigs on the farms and "black and white cows, with milk and cream cans at the railway station; a small bank balance and the return of friendship with the local bank manager — all these in addition to pleasant, comfortable homes surrounded with trees and contented families and with a feeling that there is nothing like rural life."[8]

It was probably the honest expression of a man nursing a long-suppressed desire for a relatively carefree way of rural living and the security afforded by a well ordered family farm.

In less than a year, the Lethbridge-Nobleford district had its first district agriculturist, and it was not difficult to recognize the fine hand of Charles Noble in one of the earliest public efforts by the newcomer. It took the form of a meeting at Nobleford, called to consider the organization of a Better Farming Club. The March day was cold and snow was drifting, but seventy-five people attended. The recently appointed agriculturist, M. L. Freng, was present to talk about diversified farming and advise every farmer to aim to have enough livestock to return the amount of revenue needed to cover family living expenses. The general idea was that the hens would pay for the family clothing and the pigs and cows would buy the groceries.

Mr. Noble was nodding his head in approval, and then he took the platform to discuss the topic always close to his heart, namely soils and tillage. On that subject, his judgment was regarded like a ruling from the Supreme Court, and nobody argued.

He was visibly pleased at the creation of a Better Farming Club to promote agricultural education and improved practices. He promised all the help within his power, but what he must have realized by this time was that nobody in the club needed help as much as he did. Mountain Horse had been wrong in his forecast that next year would be better for farming. The dry weather pattern continued through 1921 and 1922. Alberta wheat averaged only 10.4 bushels per acre in the former year and 11.3 bushels in the latter, and it was being sold in both years for less than eighty cents a bushel, while binders were still priced at $300 to $350.

But as Mr. Noble was quick to explain: "Our temporary losses have by no means been due entirely to dry seasons, but from the fact that in very materially increasing acreage we have departed from the careful summerfallow methods that had always gotten us results in dry years prior to the war."[9] Stated on another occasion and in another way: "Had we not been urged on in the much needed production for the war effort, we would have taken two years instead of one to break the land. Then with sod well rotted, the 1920 crop on the same land might easily have been doubled."

The uninvited presence of that omnipotent being, the receiver, produced no miracles. Instead of financial improvement, the Foundation's position deteriorated with a net loss of $51,000 in the two years of receivership, and creditors were again howling like hounds on a chase.

At the end of 1921, the Merchants Bank was being taken over by the Bank of Montreal, and Charlie Noble had a new financial master. He had no complaint about the new bank's readiness to finance current seeding operations, nor did he blame the bankers for their insistence that advances so made for current operations would have preference over payments on account of earlier mortgages. That was fair enough, but certain of the various other creditor parties did not agree. The American bondholders, in Mr. Noble's own words, "then unwisely undertook to force the bank to advance some $50,000 [for] payment of interest by starting foreclosure and I was the victim."[10]

Knowing the mood of the bondholders, Mr. Noble tried to find a plan that would "head off" foreclosure. There was only a remote hope of selling the huge farm to eastern or overseas capitalists, but it was considered. There was more chance of carrying out a proposal he had long entertained, of breaking the holdings into family-sized units and selling or renting them, equipped. It seemed likely that many of Mr. Noble's employees would seize such a chance to start farming for themselves. The proposal called for subdividing Grand View Farm one year and the Cameron the next. The bank was encouraging the idea and indicating willingness to finance the tenants or purchasers.[11] But foreclosure proceedings made public on March 6, 1923, interfered, and the plan died before it was born.

"The death knoll of the Noble Foundation has been sounded in the foreclosure application made to Mr. Justice McCarthy yesterday on behalf of the first debenture holders," the newspapers reported, adding that, "Judge McCarthy has reserved judgment but it is practically assured that he will allow the application. The motion was made by A. H. Goodall representing Henry Carstens, Seattle trustee for the first debenture holders who have a claim against the Noble Foundation of approximately $700,000."[12]

Carstens had instituted the action against the Foundation two years previously, but the proceedings were stayed and the Bankers' Trust Company, acting for the holders of the second debentures, was awarded a receivership for two years. But in spite of the receiver's best efforts, he failed to overcome the unyielding forces of shrinking prices for farm products, continuing high costs, and dry years.

A few days after the Carstens application, it was announced that foreclosure on the Noble Foundation land had been granted, thereby leaving the holders of the second mortgage with a first claim upon the other chattels.[13]

Noble Foundation property transferred to the new owners following the foreclosure included 27,588.31 acres in the various farms — about 43 sections or 172 quarter sections listed — and 51 village lots in Nobleford.[14]

The "walls were tumbling" but they were not all down yet. After another four weeks of anguish for Charles Noble, Mr. Justice Walsh granted the application made, also in Calgary, by R. B. Bennett, K.C., on behalf of the Royal Trust Company. The Royal Trust, having absorbed the Bankers' Trust which held the mortgage of $500,000, was now authorized to take possession of the other chattels.[15]

What a cruel test of human fibre. "Other chattels" meant almost everything remaining. As son Shirley noted: "Dad had pledged everything but his household furniture — even his fine home in Nobleford went."[16]

"The curtain has finally wrung down for the Noble Foundation," a reporter wrote with evident sorrow. The village of Nobleford wore an expression of sadness because the Noble farming successes were sources of community pride. Of course there were traces of jealousy, but Charles Noble belonged to the village which he had founded and the farming district which he had brought to fame and his friends were not deserting him now. He had earned local loyalty. Unlike many men of wealth and fame, the chief never lost the common touch and never ceased to be a good neighbor.

The people who won foreclosure soon discovered that their problems were still numerous and big. They had hoped to gain possession of the land early in the year to allow sufficient time to organize for seeding. They knew the Noble land was fertile and in the best state of tilth, with much of it ready for the drill. There had never been neglect of land, not even when economic pressures mounted, and the new owners should have been grateful for this — and for the substantial bonuses of 5,000 acres of well prepared summerfallow ready for cropping and more than 3,000 acres of winter rye showing excellent growth and vigor.

The finance company gaining possession of the Foundation's livestock and machinery on the strength of the second mortgage was not obliged to act in haste, but the new owners of the land knew they had to act with lightning speed if they were to make all the proper arrangements for seeding. They possessed no power and no equipment, and a feeling of resentment in the community certainly did not reduce their problems.

The result was general confusion at a time when most farmers were starting to work their land. At this point a committee of American bankers and businessmen arrived on the scene, and after a couple of days of contemplation about the future of the property in which they had a new interest, they were reported to have made the less-than-profound decision that "the former lands of the Noble Foundation should be kept in a continued state of cultivation." The expression of wisdom did nothing to reduce the pre-seeding confusion. Helpfully, however, Fred Hutchings, a representative of Alberta Pacific Grain Company living at Barons, was named to manage the new corporation which had been formed hurriedly by the bondholders, and Howard Roberts was chosen to be his assistant.

The immediate hope was to find local farmers with a surplus of power and machinery who would agree to lease portions of the big farm. The managers promised "very favorable leases," and were able to interest fifteen parties in renting. Even a few residents of the village undertook to buy or borrow horses, harness, and secondhand machines to become renters and weekend operators on what was formerly Noble land. But what fifteen renters took was only a small part of the great land holdings, and what the hard-pressed managers were unable to rent, they were obliged to seed and farm with hired help and such equipment as they were able to borrow from the Royal Trust Company's recently acquired stockpile.

While seeding was in progress, machinery and livestock were being sold at both Grand View and the Cameron. The biggest single sale consisted of 116 horses — about one fifth of the total number — taken by Durno and Smith for resale in Calgary. Sales continued throughout the summer, and every item seen leaving the premises — especially if it were one of Mr. Noble's beloved horses — was like a stab at his heart.

It was for him a bitter and trying experience. How could it be otherwise, seeing his farming enterprise with a $2½ million inventory vanishing to satisfy a debt totalling less than half of the amount? But months earlier, when he saw the "handwriting on the wall," he made resolve by letter to Hon. George Hoadley: "If defeat is really in store for us, it will only prove the more that all attention possible must be directed to small farms and diversified methods, and I am determined to be a good loser."[17]

A fine public image comes easily to the person being swept along on resounding waves of success, but it takes the test of tribulation to reveal true depth of character, and those people who watched Charles Noble in the agonizing months of 1923 said "he passed with the highest honors."

15
REBUILDING
THE WALL

What now? Is this the end of the road for Charlie? The questions were asked a hundred times as neighbors met in and around the village, and the response was usually about the same: "It's hard to say what he'll do now or where he'll go but he'll never farm again. Nobody would go back to farming after a beating like he took. If he stays around here, chances are he'll go back to selling real estate. He could make a living at that."

A few of Noble's employees who had acquired small allotments of shares in the Foundation — mainly foremen — became minor losers too, and their minor losses were to be regretted. But it was the chief, holding more than ninety-eight per cent of the stock of the company, who was the spectacular loser and for whom the loss could be critical. Nobody would ever try to minimize the jolt of a farming colossus coming crashing down upon its builder's head. The memory could be expected to last like that of a bad nightmare.

There was no consolation or glory in being the first person in history to have owned 33,000 acres of good farm land one day and none — not even an acre — the next. Millionaire Noble was literally left with nothing but his family, his furniture, and his love of soil. The cynics, to be sure, said he probably went bankrupt with his pockets full of cash, but there was not the slightest evidence that such was the case. Any way it was assessed, it was a cruel blow, and the neighbors who stopped on the plank sidewalk or in the company store to swap opinions were right in their conclusions that there was no reason to expect that a man who had suffered so much mental agony and loss of property during those recent months would attempt a comeback in the same area of business.

But Noble was made of sturdy stuff, with an uncommon stubborn streak running through it. Sure, he had suffered, but he had no intention of surrendering to circumstances or abandoning agriculture. His dedication to the soil was like his loyalty to his church, unchanged. Whether he was thinking in terms of history or not, he had an excellent practical concept of it. Isn't history simply a record of human experiences, good and bad? Noble was well aware that his experience had cost him dearly. In other words, he had a huge investment in farm experience, and his only chance of recovering from it or profiting by it was in staying with his initial choice of occupation.

He was now exactly fifty years of age, celebrating the anniversary on May 16 by watching the final stages in the disintegration of his empire. He knew that recovery would be slow and for a man who had built and directed the biggest farming concern in Canada, it would be exasperating. But Charlie Noble's intentions were never in doubt. He would farm, but farm by somewhat different guidelines. Drawing upon his investment in history and experience, he would revise his goals; he would hope to turn some of his earlier mistakes to benefit by guarding against repetition; he would farm less and farm better. Just how much less, however, remained to be seen. He had become an advocate of the relatively small family farm, but it was a big farm that had brought temporary ruin and it was unlikely that the challenge of success with a bigger-than-average farm would leave a stubborn man alone.

Charles Noble had never known an idle day, and even in this troubled period when his farm had been snatched from him, he was not idle. He took stock of his intangible assets over which the court had no jurdisdiction. Physical assets could be seized, but he had the strength and will to work, and even after bankruptcy, his reputation for honesty remained. Almost at once the new owners asked him to assist in the sale of chattels such as horses and machinery that had been his own. Without bitterness, he accepted, knowing full well that a salary of $4,000 a year would prove very useful at this point.

At the same time, a bank loan given freely allowed him to pay rent on the fine Nobleford house which had been the family home and in which the Nobles could continue to reside. The loan permitted, also, the purchase of some aged horses and secondhand machinery, thus placing him in a position to be one of the renters of the Grand View land. As his son Shirley reported: "Then, with two teen-aged sons and what other help he could afford, he rented three sections of the Grand View farm on a crop share basis, with an option to purchase."[1]

The press, while reporting the arrangement to rent three sections, answered the question that had been on many lips by stating that: "Mr. C. S. Noble's presence will be felt in the community.... He will demonstrate that some paying crops can be grown, other than grain."[2]

Then, ironically, after several dry years that contributed to the Foundation's failure, the weather mood reversed and everything planted in 1923 grew luxuriantly. Wheat planted on what had been Foundation fields yielded between forty and forty-eight bushels per acre, and the new owners reaped returns far beyond their expectations or earned deserts. Crops on the three sections rented by Mr. Noble and his sons — mostly rye — paid off well, providing a new financial base upon which to build and expand. For the entire province of Alberta, the average yield of wheat was twenty-eight bushels per acre, a figure that was second only to the average of thirty-one bushels in 1915.

But for farmers generally, the overriding question of 1923 concerned marketing of the big crop. Local sales of wheat at Lethbridge were still at less than eighty-five cents per bushel, rye at less than forty-five cents a bushel, and oats at thirty cents. Farmers across the West, increasingly distrustful of the open market and Winnipeg Grain Exchange, had begged for a government-appointed wheat board to handle the crop in a national pool. Early in the season there was an indication of getting one resembling the board of 1919. But that hope vanished, and farm organizations became instantly vocal in challenging growers to act for themselves. Farmers were angry, and the idea of forming their own marketing pools found widespread support. Meetings were called on short notices and debates were often heated.

The country's wheat was in head, and many binder reels were turning before the farmers made the bold and courageous decision in favor of a hurried drive to obtain producer contracts that would bind a minimum of fifty per cent of the province's wheat acreage to marketing pools for a five-year period. The week of August 20 was set for the sign-up campaign in Alberta, and although the workers combing the farming country with a religious zeal failed to win the fifty per cent goal, the total acreage committed was close to the objective and the leaders decided to proceed with the biggest cooperative marketing plan ever undertaken in Canada.

Saskatchewan, in starting its campaign later and failing to obtain the wanted fifty per cent of the province's wheat acreage, decided to delay the final organization until the next year, 1924. But the Alberta farmers were in business.

Charles Noble was not one of the original signers but there were reasons. In the first place, he did not own any land at that time. Secondly, his five-year future was about as uncertain as a Hollywood marriage, and finally, he had become a grower of rye more than wheat.

His infatuation with winter rye began with a recognition of the multiple advantages to be derived from a fall-planted grain crop. Basically, he was searching for a means of holding the prairie soil against drifting during spring and early summer when fields are often without a protective covering. An autumn-planted grain crop could be expected to furnish the spring cover and more. It might furnish some autumn and spring grazing for horses and cattle without injury to itself. It would choke out weeds like Russian thistles, and because of advancement and maturity by early August, it would be almost sure of escaping the damage later crops frequently suffered from fall frosts. Finally, by extending its growing season over a larger period of time, it made it possible for the farmer to use hired help more efficiently.

Winter rye could do all this and Charlie Noble became enthusiastic. Speaking to the delegates attending the Irrigation Conference at Lethbridge in July, 1921, Noble could say that the Foundation's land had "almost escaped" the growing menace of soil drifting, and the two principal reasons were to be found in his lumpy-surface technique in cultivation and, secondly, the extensive use of winter rye.

On Noble's recommendations, winter rye's popularity spread quickly across the southwest. Only the limited supplies of seed prevented it from spreading even faster. Farmers were pleased and reported the rye to be their most reliable crop. Even the provincial Department of Agriculture mounted the "band-wagon" and went to great lengths to promote what some of the Lethbridge farmers were calling "Charlie's crop."

Always searching for new crops and new varieties, Noble was attracted by a new kind he encountered in travels in the United States, Rosen rye with inherited Russian hardiness, and introduced it from Michigan in 1918. He established the new strain in his seed plots and sold it extensively until another variety, Dakold, was demonstrating superior worth.

In adopting new farming practices, Noble was always a leader, and when he was starting over again after the financial crash, he stepped back into the forefront as though he had never vacated it. Winter rye and winter wheat afforded him useful vehicles for the return. It was his high regard for winter rye with its visible advantages in the struggles against drought and drifting soil that led Noble to winter wheat and left him nursing a typical enthusiasm.

Wheat had always enjoyed better markets than rye, probably always would. Winter wheat would be able to blanket the spring and summer soil as well as winter rye, and if hardy varieties of the former were available to growers, winter wheat would almost certainly find high favor in that southern section of Alberta. So Charlie Noble reasoned.

It had been discovered as early as 1902 when E. E. Thompson imported a carload of winter wheat called Nebraska Red — later known as Alberta Red — that the crop could be grown with marginal success in the region. Farmers recognized advantages, including a relatively high yield when it grew, and wanted it. Apparently, it enjoyed a period of popularity but there were too many disappointments. As Charlie Noble told it, the crop "was given up some years ago because of frequent winter killings and resulting poor stands and weeds. But with the introduction of a new winter hardy variety, a revival of earlier practices has begun. Five years ago we secured from Macdonald College in Quebec, one bushel of their improved Kharkov 22 M.C. winter wheat. This variety had already given promise of being very winter hardy and our experience with it to date has been entirely satisfactory in this respect."[3]

Noble's new success with winter wheat, which was winning attention across the southwest, came, however, from his revised technique in cultivating and planting as much as from the hardy variety of his introduction. When he recognized the need for a more reliable winter wheat, he set out with characteristic resolution to find it or fashion it by whatever means was necessary. By his reasoning, there had to be some relationship between the state of cultivation in a field and a wheat plant's ability to survive a hard winter. Having heard that experimentalists in Montana were entertaining similar thoughts, he was anxious to know if they had any information that might be useful to him and other Canadians. He would pay them a visit.

A reporter overtook him when he was setting out on a Montana tour and wrote: "C. S. Noble of Nobleford, one of the best informed farmers of Southern Alberta, will leave for Montana in the morning where he will make an intensive study of winter wheat with a view of introducing it on a fairly large scale on his holdings here. Mr. Noble reaffirmed his faith in winter wheat as one of the coming crops in this country."[4]

When the reporter reached him, he was carrying a sample of his Kharkov 22 M.C. and speculating that the field from which it came would yield over thirty bushels to the acre "without another drop of rain." And then he had something to add about reliability of the crop, saying that: "Where land is well summerfallowed and the seed is sound, there is no reason why a good crop of winter wheat should not be gathered. I would like to see it pushed more.... That is why I am going down there [to Montana] to learn more about it."

It appeared that the exchange of ideas in Montana proved profitable for the conferring individuals from both sides, and Noble returned with a conviction that he needed a new kind of seed drill, one that would give wider spacing to the planted rows and deposit the seed in soil at the bottom of small furrows or trenches made by the drill discs or shoes. He had already experimented with something of the kind and believed it would furnish shelter for young wheat plants and the ridged condition would help to check the sweep of eroding winds.

Arriving back from Montana, he found his winter wheat ready to be cut and his seed for the next crop ready for planting. The stand of maturing wheat looked better than ever and the summerfallow was in fine shape for the seed. But before giving instructions for planting, Noble was determined to reconstruct a seed drill that would accomplish what became known as furrow seeding.

His friends in Montana were working on something of the kind and produced a drill using either single discs or double discs for making the desired seed rows twelve inches apart. When the single disc was employed, each one had to be set at a sharp angle to open the furrow rows. With the double disc arrangement, one disc was set ahead of the other, both throwing the soil in opposite directions and leaving a trench in which the seed would be drilled with fairly high protecting ridges between the furrows or seed rows.

Noble's objective was the same, but he chose to work with the hoe type of drill instead of the disc type. He welded metal wings on the sides of each hoe, about two inches back from the point. In the field, these wings could cut the desired furrows and leave the soil piled in high ridges with the seed planted in the furrow bottoms.

That was not the end of the Noble invention. He wanted to follow the drill with a packer that would press the soil over the seed in each furrow without spoiling or reducing the ridges. How was that to be done? It called again for Noble's ingenuity. To make such a packer with suitable packing wheels, he began by fixing eighteen-inch disc blades in pairs, one inch apart at the rims, and filling the intervening space with concrete. With the weighted discs or wheels mounted and attached carefully behind the drill so each packer wheel would run exactly in the furrow where it belonged, the seedbed could be packed without disturbance to the ridges which were in place to break the wind and catch snow.

New drills were completed in time for the August seeding of some 600 acres of the winter wheat, and Noble was pleased and confident. The experiments thus far, he said, had convinced him that this crop had a larger place than it had gained, especially in the drier sections. It should have a place on every farm where there was a desire to cut down the rush of spring and harvest work and retard drifting. Farmers in the area were listening to him, as they always did, and so was the agricultural editor of the *Lethbridge Herald* who then advised farmers generally to obtain at least a bushel of Kharkov 22 M.C. for the purpose of testing it and growing a better supply of seed.[5]

By 1927, Noble's Kharkov 22 M.C. — "probably the hardiest variety known" as he stated — was indeed extending the same soil protection that his winter rye had been doing, and he could report seven consecutive years without severe winter killing. "Last year," he added, "one 340-acre field averaged fifty-six bushels." It sounded like the Charlie Noble of other years when he was the biggest supplier of rye seed in the south; now, in 1927, he was the biggest supplier of winter wheat.

Noble's recovery from the financial blow of 1923 was rapid and convincing. In 1927, after the family had lived for a couple of years in Calgary, the elegant Nobleford home with indoor swimming pool — probably the first in southern Alberta — and rich in family memories was bought back and again became the Noble home. In the meantime, four sections of Grand View Farm, including the buildings and some of the best soil, were repurchased at a price of thirty-two dollars an acre, on crop payments, and in 1930, eight sections of the Cameron Ranch land were bought back. That made twelve sections returned to the Noble name, and although such an expanse of land far exceeded the bounds of the conventional family farms about which Mr. Noble had been talking in approving terms, the new enterprise was indeed a family farm because with Mr. Noble and members of his family as co-owners, it was incorporated as Noble Farms, Limited. Everybody was in it, including the two sons and one daughter, Alleen.[6]

The new farming enterprise — big by comparison with the average prairie farms, small by comparison with the Noble Foundation farms of bygone years — led Hon. Duncan Marshall, ever an admirer, to write: "Mr. Noble was [beginning again] where he was about 1905, except that he had a world of experience, and few farmers have ever profited more by what they have come through than this courageous fighter for crops on dry land. He always believed there were better methods of dealing with drought and soil drifting than we knew of, and he pursued every avenue of information and experience that opened to him."[7]

16
THE GREAT PARADE
OF COMBINES

Nothing in the history of grain fields did more to turn things around workwise than the adoption of the harvester-combines. It served to terminate the annual harvesters' excursions which brought thousands of easterners to help in crop recovery and gave most of them their first glimpse of the West at bargain rates; it retired the weary stookers and gave blistered hands and aching backs a chance to heal; and it was the means of sending a quarter of a million binders and a few thousand threshing machines to the scrap piles and junkyards from which there was no resurrection.

Charles Noble did not invent the grain combine and was not the first western Canadian to use one. But he was the first to adopt the machine on a large scale and the first to present it properly for public viewing. It was a typical Noble performance.

California witnessed the longest strides in combine development, but frontier inventors in many parts of the grain country, including the Canadian West, were making models and stumbling upon useful ideas that were ultimately incorporated into efficient, modern machines. A Calgarian, J. Clove, built what became known as Clove's Travelling Thresher about 1912 and had it working in grain fields near Alderson and Suffield in 1915. Later in that same season, Clove displayed it for the United Farmers of Alberta in Calgary.[1]

"The travelling thresher is just what its name signifies," the press informed. "It is a thresher equipped with an automobile motor and the principle upon which it operates is that instead of the grain having to be brought to the machine ... the machine goes to the grain. It moves through the field under its own power and threshes from the stooks. One man drives the machine and looks after the motive power and another attends to the separator arrangement. Four men at the stooks just pitchfork the sheaves into the travelling elevator which carries them up into the machine where they are threshed on the spot."

In California a manufacturers' contest seemed to arise between Charles Holt and Daniel Best, largely to see who could build the bigger machine. Best made one requiring a heavy steam tractor or seventy-five mules to pull it. Holt followed with a combine cutting a fifty-foot swath.

The threshing mechanism in the earliest combines was driven by a big bull wheel, but by 1906 auxiliary engines were being installed and by 1911 the first self-propelled combines were introduced.

Calgary's J. Clove may have had the first harvester-combine in Alberta, but C. P. J. Shand and Harry Edmonds of Spy Hill, Saskatchewan, brought a combine to their province in 1909 or 1910. It was a Holt with a twelve-foot cutting bar and was pulled by a 30-60 Hart-Parr gasoline tractor. It probably inspired amusement as much as admiration.

The first combine that Charles Noble saw in Alberta was in the machinery display at the celebrated Dry Farming Congress of 1912. It was a Holt machine, described as "Holt Brothers' Sidehill Combined Harvester and Thresher," and it was in motion daily during the Congress, inside the Lethbridge racetrack. Three machines of the kind were owned by Alberta farmers at that time, one at Tilley, one at Strathmore, and one at Bassano.[2]

Almost all the combine harvesters of that period were made in the United States. The Massey Harris machine was one of the leading exceptions. That Canadian company had a "stripper harvester" on the market in 1901, a miniature of what was to come. A more advanced model, the No. 1 Reaper-Combine, appeared in 1910, and a still more mature creation, the No. 5 Reaper-Thresher, appeared in 1922. One of the latter was lent to the new experimental station at Swift Current for testing. The station later bought the machine and used it to demonstrate the new technique in the prairie grain fields. The company then adopted a policy of lending combines to selected farmers for testing and demonstration. The public response was favorable, and farmers saw where they could make big savings in the cost of harvesting. One of these machines was turned over to Charlie Noble.

Noble bought his first combine — a Case — and was then awarded the Massey Harris on a lend-lease basis. That was in 1926, and with gasoline tractors pulling the two machines and his two sons operating them, he was well pleased with the performance, sufficiently pleased that in the next year, 1927, he added four more combines to the fleet, three Holts and another Massey Harris. When a large party of visitors drove to the Nobleford farm on August 11, they saw harvest operations starting in a 1300-acre field of Kharkov 22 M.C. winter wheat, the variety Mr. Noble had obtained from its breeder, Macdonald College of Quebec. The stand of wheat was magnificent, appearing good for a yield of between forty and sixty bushels to the acre. The crop was not quite ready for straight combining, and Mr. Noble was testing another very new machine called a "header or swather" which would place cut grain in swaths where it would remain until it hardened and from where it would be picked up and threshed by the combine. Farmers of later years knew all about that technique.

Thus, the swather was another very important innovation making its local appearance on the Nobleford soil and soon to find general acceptance. But that 1927 autumn proved to be unusually wet and unusually exasperating to people with big crops to be recovered. Delays were serious, and both the traditional threshing machines and the newer combines experienced them alike. The people who enjoyed the most luck were those like Noble who had winter wheat which came to maturity early and escaped at least part of the prolonged wet spell. It was the kind of harvest that seemed to test human endurance and drive a few threshermen mad, best illustrated by the fact that Noble, who began the harvest at the end of July, did not finish until after the snow came in November.

The harvest experience was dismal, but the *Lethbridge Herald* found something cheerful and significant about which to write. Before indulging in some pertinent reviewing for the benefit of readers, the news writers declared for the record that "a feature of this year's harvest is the advent of the combine in fairly large numbers," then pointed to the evidence found near at hand. "One of the greatest demonstrations of the combine this season has been on the Noble farm at Nobleford. At that point, made famous by the world record crop of 1916, C. S. Noble is cashing in on his faith in Southern Alberta. Following an unprofitable adventure in Cameron Ranch land during the war when the cry for 'greater production' caused him to plunge into one of the greatest farming ventures in the history of the West with the result that a large fortune was wiped out, Mr. Noble is this year staging a comeback that is the talk of the whole south country."

It was in truth a further triumph for perseverance. Four rather dispirited years had passed since the cruel force of bankruptcy had obliterated the former farming empire, and for much of that time, the man who had been its victim seemed to be cut off from the public gaze. Now, as with another wave of fortune's wand, he was back in the agricultural forefront and being pursued by reporters who recognized news in the most modern farming methods and in "the largest battery of combines ever seen in one field in Canada."[3]

There was added newspaper and public interest in what gave indication at that time of being another Noble crop of world record yield. Secretly, Mr. Noble was hoping the prognosticators were right and that his beloved winter wheat would return a bushelage big enough to break his own Noble Foundation record of fifty-four bushels and twenty-three pounds of wheat per acre on a field exceeding 1,000 acres. That was memory's trophy from the brave year of 1916. The current crop giving so much promise was being grown on the same land and in exactly the same field that had given the proud record eleven years earlier; and as in the earlier year, farmers and urban people were driving to Nobleford to see this highly publicized stand of grain. This time, however, it was not Marquis wheat but rather Kharkov 22 M.C., but looking very much like a crop coming close to perfection, made impressive by big and well filled heads, freedom from weeds, uniformity of growth, and every plant growing almost to Charlie Noble's armpits.

The earliest combining on a 340-acre portion of the big field — done before the rains became damaging — strengthened the hope for another record by yielding fifty-six bushels and forty pounds per acre. If that average could be maintained, it would be a most convincing record, and the Lethbridge Board of Trade, always looking for an opportunity to further publicize the goodness of southern Alberta soil and climate, returned to promote public interest and excitement. But the damp autumn weather spoiled what might have been a football-like display of patriotic fervor. Before the balance of the 1,300-acre field could be combined, some of the wheat had shelled, some was consumed by mice, and some of the heavy heads fell to the ground with the result that kernels sprouted. The big field was definitely out of contention for international yield honors. When finally threshed, the returns showed an average of "approximately fifty bushels per acre," which for most growers would still be a momentous occurrence. As it was, most of Noble's Kharkov wheat from that crop went into storage for the seed trade he had good reason to anticipate.

Noble, over the years, made many crop records and they brought him well deserved satisfaction, but he was still more concerned about accuracy and honest reporting than with the glory that would come with more successes. When rumors and certain news items had it that his big field yielded sixty bushels of winter wheat per acre and had thereby qualified for another world record in the category of large area production, he hastened to write to the press to declare that it was not so. Just as readily, he told that some of his neighbors were in that year showing bigger yields from their Marquis wheat than he had managed to achieve with his winter variety.[4]

As he explained it, the standing crop that had excited visions of another world record — perhaps sixty bushels to the acre — eluded him like many things in life, including big fish and fortunes. "Unfortunately, the story of the balance of the 1,350 acres is like the story of the big fish the fellow caught. He got the fish where he could see it and note its exact size; but while helping it from the water into the boat, something happened and that particular fish was lost."

In his ardent promotion of winter wheat, he might have omitted to tell that his Marquis and his neighbors' Marquis had in that year yielded fully as well as his Kharkov. But to his credit, he chose to make full disclosure, even though it would probably injure his sales of the Kharkov winter wheat seed.

The first two sections of Cameron Ranch property to be bought back by the Nobles were purchased in January, 1929,[5] and at harvest time later in the year, visitors saw nine combines working in unison, one behind the other like a train of Red River carts on the old Fort Edmonton Trail. At least five of these machines, as recalled by Edward Fraser, Mr. Noble's nephew who was driving a Hart Parr tractor and pulling a Holt combine, were his own property. The other combines were on loan for testing and demonstration, but working in close proximity to one another, they presented a sight that many Albertans wanted to see and made some of the noise, no doubt, that produced the "Roar of the Twenties."

Fraser, who was raised at Claresholm and attended the Claresholm School of Agriculture, remembered that two of the nine combines were Holts, one was a John Deere, one was an International, at least one was a Massey Harris, and the most memorable was the giant Harris, a California-made machine cutting a swath thirty-four feet wide. It was the biggest combine in service in Canada at that time, and when a Lethbridge reporter made an inspection, it was cutting one hundred acres of crop per day and threshing 3,000 bushels of wheat.[6]

After giving long service in the Noble fields, the supersize Harris combine was sent to find permanent rest at the Reynolds Museum at Wetaskiwin.

It was not quite consistent with the arguments Mr. Noble had been advancing on behalf of horses and mules in the late years of the Foundation, but circumstances had changed considerably in the postwar years. With the rather sudden adoption of the harvester-combine as a substitute for the grain binder, the draft animals of the farm received another set-back.

To haul grain from the nine combines to elevators at Turin on the Lethbridge Northern branch line or at Nobleford, no fewer than twenty trucks were required. It would have taken more than a hundred horses to have performed the same service. But with the advanced degree of mechanization came a new and unexpected hazard, that of fire in the grain fields.

The harvest of 1927 was delayed and marred by wet weather. There was neither the danger nor even the possibility of fire in the damp fields, but by contrast, the autumn of 1929 was extremely dry, excellent for combining or threshing, and as Charles Noble discovered, conducive to burning. "Never before in the history of Southern Alberta harvesting," he said, "has the fire hazard in grain fields been as serious."[7] The hot exhausts from nine gasoline tractors pulling combines and twenty motor trucks, all passing over the dry stubble, were the source of greatest danger.

After seeing one fire started from the exhaust of a truck and burning fifteen acres of standing crop and a much bigger acreage of stubble on the Cameron land, Noble confessed fright. "I thought at one time a whole section of wheat was going to go," he said. He acted promptly, as he was wont to do, called for an end of smoking in the harvest fields, and telephoned the editor of the *Lethbridge Herald,* urging him to sound a warning to farmers over the area and advise all possible precautions before there was a tragedy. The editor acknowledged gratitude on behalf of the farmers.

Edward Fraser believed that this was the first time that nine combines were photographed working together anywhere in Canada. In any case, these machines which were slashing the traditional number of harvest workers and cutting general costs were winning instant popularity. It is presumed that there were not more than a dozen combines in addition to Noble's two in southern Alberta in 1926. In the next year, there were an estimated 75 in operation south of Calgary and in 1929, something over 500. It was still only the beginning. In 1931, according to Canada Year Books, farmers in Manitoba, Saskatchewan, and Alberta owned 8,917 combines, and by 1971, their total in the area stood at 127,509. The latter total represented 73 combines for every one hundred farms, and it also represented seventy-eight percent of the combines in Canada.

When the full story of the grain combine in western Canada's grain fields is written, Charles Noble must be presented as one of those leading the dramatic parade.

17
DRIFTING SOIL AND ITS EVIL COMPANIONS

For Charles Sherwood Noble, neither drought, economic disaster, nor drifting soil was a totally new experience. He had pioneer encounters with all three of the evils, having seen wind erosion in the Dakotas at the beginning of the century and severe drought in Alberta in 1910, 1918, and 1919, when total precipitation and average crop yields for the Lethbridge area were lower than in the driest years of the '30s. And, surely, his private financial crisis terminating in bankruptcy in 1923 was enough to make the reverses of the '30s seem no more than repetition. But never had he nor any other human seen all three of the destroying monsters coming together with such ferocity as in the memorable decade that followed 1929.

Arriving hand in hand like scheming companions, dry weather, drifting soil, and economic failure made entry or re-entry upon the western scene in 1929, when the average yield of wheat in the region of Charlie Noble's farms was less than ten bushels per acre and in the entire south of Alberta, less than eight bushels.

If the Great Depression — settling in as if coming to stay — had an official date of entry, it had to be Friday, October 18, 1929, when unprecedented fear and wild selling seized the commanding New York Stock Exchange, generating a frenzy that travelled at the speed of lightning to other international trading centers and brought ruin to thousands of investors.

The period of warning was brief. Stock markets displayed a perceptible uneasiness for a few days before the crash, but markets were known as temperamental things at any time and a depressed trade was normally followed in short order by adjustment, rally, and recovery. Stock exchanges depended upon the constant antics of the "bulls" trying to drive prices higher and the "bears" driving them lower. But here was something ominously different; even the most seasoned speculators were shocked by this "Black Friday" performance when nearly all traders, without hiding their fears, wanted to be sellers. With the "bears" in command and the "bulls" in disorderly retreat, the New York market witnessed the most frantic spell of liquidation in stock exchange history. As a result of crashing prices, $2½ billion in paper values disappeared during the day.

Investment banks and other powerful financial institutions turned to heavy buying in an attempt to restore confidence, but Tuesday, October 29, saw a repetition of the panic selling. Wall Street had never recorded such a wild opening; 3,259,000 shares changed hands at depressed prices in the first thirty minutes. Wheat prices on the Winnipeg market fell seven cents, and the financial world was plunging into trouble from which it would not free itself for almost ten years.

Editors, writers, and politicians tried to be cheerful and dutifully proclaimed confidence that complete economic recovery and unprecedented prosperity were "just around the corner." Their intentions were good but their prophetic senses were hopelessly inadequate, and the evasive "corner" was still more remote than the "experts" imagined.

Farm products did not escape the long sweep of price decline, and in spite of the hollow expressions of optimism sounded with almost monotonous regularity, the price of wheat continued on its downward and ruinous way for more than three years before reaching its lowest point in history. It wasn't easy to be honestly cheerful as unemployment soared and relief measures had to be adopted on a broader scale than ever.

Most debts could not be collected; farm taxes went unpaid; school teachers congratulated themselves on their luck when they were able to collect their modest wages; and the World Grain Show, scheduled to be presented at Regina in 1932, was postponed until 1933 in the hope that conditions would improve in the meantime. Alberta's unemployed, in December, 1932, conducted a "Hunger March" to Edmonton where a thousand hostile people demonstrated at the legislative building and clashed with police. Thirty-five of the marchers and two of the police officers were injured.

Another army of disgruntled men, travelling in their "private freight cars" or "riding the rods," made their way to Ottawa at a time that coincided with the politically important Imperial Economic Conference for which Prime Minister R. B. Bennett was the Canadian host.

It was on December 16, 1932 — just a few days after Herman Trelle of Wembley in the Peace River area won the World Wheat Championship in Chicago — that No. 1 Northern wheat made distressing history by recording its lowest all-time trading price at Winnipeg, namely 39⅞ cents per bushel.

And at country points, mainly because of the cost of rail transportation, the prices paid to growers were considerably lower. A wagonload of the No. 1 Northern wheat for local sale on that December day would have brought twenty-four cents a bushel at Lethbridge or sixteen cents a bushel at Peace River.

Other farm products were making similarly dismal records. The farmer selling at Lethbridge in the same month of December could have hoped for nothing better than 8½ cents a bushel for oats, 13½ cents a bushel for barley, $2.70 per hundred pounds for butcher steers, $3.75 per hundred for bacon pigs, and 8 cents a pound for dressed turkeys of best quality. Sales did not leave much cash for the purchase of Christmas presents or Christmas groceries. The farmer whose hens were laying in that winter season when most farm hens were taking their holidays might have captured the price prize of the year, 28 cents a dozen for eggs of first quality, although eggs of the equivalent grade had sold for as low as 3 cents a dozen when supplies were abundant in the previous May. And in their feverish 1932 quest for cash with which to buy necessities for the home, southern Alberta farmers sold over 10,000 horses for shipment to a horse meat plant at Butte, Montana, realizing an average price of less than $10 per head.

Charlie Noble and his family were never reduced to the necessity of eating gophers or using roasted barley as a substitute for coffee, but an 8,000-acre farm which could be profitable in good times when both crop yields and prices were favorable was almost sure to be a ruinous liability — like a slow racehorse — when returns would not even pay taxes and interest on capital debt. To keep the farm operational, Noble was obliged to borrow again and worry again about the uncertainties of the future of farming in the semiarid region. The only thing that would save him from the same fate of bankruptcy was the lesson about the need for extreme caution and thrift carried over from the previous bout with debts and dry years.

Drought and depressed prices were bad enough, and a few writers concluded finally that the prairie West was becoming a desert. One of them suggested abandoning wheat and bringing back the buffalo. "The Golden Age of wheat has ended," he wrote. But the steadfast people like Noble knew that both soil moisture and better prices would return sooner or later. What Noble believed to be the most dangerous phenomenon, because it might become the most lasting, was the incidence of soil drifting, mounting annually rather than diminishing. He recalled the sad spectacle of good soil being lifted off the fields in Kansas and the Dakotas and formed a fear and hatred of it. He was shocked at the first meaningful appearance of soil drifting in the Lethbridge region in 1916 and warned that the losses even then were greater than casual observers realized. It was consistent with a point made by soil specialists at the Lethbridge Experimental Station many years later that soil losses from wind are likely to reach five tons per acre before owners become conscious of the trouble.

Noble had lost none of his feeling for soil. The loam in his fields was still like a living thing, responding to food and care. Now this "creature's" health and vigor were being threatened by a new and merciless enemy, wind erosion. It was an enemy that did not appear until soils lost much of their original plant fibre or humus and were left with finely pulverized and exposed surfaces.

There was no doubt; the bare and highly cultivated summerfallows invited erosion. The once-favored "dust mulch" summerfallows popularized in the years of H. W. Campbell had to be abandoned. As soil fibre was gradually lost, soil surfaces required some compensating protection to blunt the force of the winds. Charlie Noble, an experimentalist by nature, was one of the first Canadians to search for a cure that would be compatible with profitable production. He gave up the use of the disc as a cultivating implement and tried the duckfoot cultivator with widely spaced shovels or bottoms, using the latter in such a way as to bring lumps to the surface and leave the fields ridged instead of smooth. In the first years of drifting, this was enough to bring stability to Noble's fields.

But with further annual losses of organic matter it was not enough, and better methods were needed to prevent the waste. Noble tried cover crops on summerfallow fields, but they were robbing the fallow land of too much of the precious moisture and the idea was abandoned.

A form of strip farming that might have been seen as an

elementary stage in developing the widely adopted strips consisted of seeding a single drill width of crop at intervals across the summerfallow fields. By 1919, Noble was attempting to reduce the force of the wind by planting these ribbons of crop at intervals of five to ten rods and making certain that they were running north and south to be at right angles to the prevailing winds. Again it could be said that until soil drifting had become more acute, these narrow strips were enough to protect the fields. But still searching for something more effective, Noble turned to growing winter rye and introduced the variety known as Rosen from Michigan. This crop, planted on the summerfallowed land in August, had enough leaf growth to protect the fields against the winds in both autumn and spring months.

P. M. Abel of the *Grain Growers' Guide* paid a special visit to the Noble farms in the spring of 1920 when the fear of soil drifting was mounting and wrote:

> The Noble Foundation, situated in the heart of the worst wind-swept area in Alberta, has sustained only slight losses due to the generous use of winter rye.... Sown after the rush of summerfallow plowing, it makes good growth before winter and collects snow. In the dry chinook country, soil blowing during the winter months is often as serious as in summer.... The result obtained on the Noble farms in 1920, from winter rye and the use of the rod cultivator is eloquent testimony of the effectiveness of these two aids in preventing soil drifting.[1]

Noble's involvement with winter rye led to his adoption of winter wheat, which had the advantage of having a more reliable market than rye while offering the equivalent ground cover in the months when blowing was most likely to occur. Again, such a measure was sufficient to hold the soil for some years after 1920. It meant that by one means or another, soil on the Noble land was being held to the chief's satisfaction, and hundreds of farmers in the south were attracted to winter rye or winter wheat.

There was still a spell during the summerfallow year, before the winter rye or winter wheat was planted, when the land surface was bare and vulnerable. The need for protection for a longer summer season brought the Lethbridge area searchers to the discovery and then the general use of strip farming in a new form. It was a simple device, but its simplicity did not prevent it from gaining a permanent place in dry land farming practice far and near. It brought fame to the Lethbridge area and the men who found the idea and shared it, men like L. P. Tuff, the Koole brothers, and Charles Noble.

That much of the best pioneer work in combating soil drifting was performed in the area of Lethbridge should not be surprising. Any prairie farming district getting less than seventeen inches of total precipitation in most years and more than the average amount of wind could hardly escape being an early candidate for soil drifting. Farmers thereabout were among the first in the West to experience the erosion menace and among the first to act resolutely against it.

L. P. Tuff, in 1915, wrote to the *Lethbridge Herald* to offer a seeding plan based on alternate strips of crop and summer-fallow. It differed from Mr. Noble's original method by advocating crop and summerfallow strips of equal width.

"A unique plan for the prevention of soil drifting has been invented by L. P. Tuff, a farmer near Lethbridge," the newspaper reported, "and the *Herald* has pleasure in reproducing a plan he has drawn."[2]

The plan showed strips of twenty rods in width, running north and south. As Tuff related the details: "These plots ... run north and south so you can see the winds get no sweep [at them] as there is stubble on the strips to be summerfallowed. I got this idea from the fact that land near stubble or sod, say for 20 [rods] out, never moves with the wind, be the wind ever so hard."

But it was for the Koole brothers, Leonard and Arie — Noble's neighbors in the nearby Monarch district — to conduct the boldest and best demonstrations on behalf of strip farming, and their names will be forever linked with the practice. The Kooles were progressive immigrants who came from Holland by way of the United States and took homestead land in the Monarch district in 1905. They hauled lumber from Fort Macleod with which to build shacks and experienced the usual range of farming hardships, including dry years and near-ruinous market prices. By 1916 — after ten years of cropping — they were seeing their soil lifting into the air and moving eastward and southeastward. With Dutch respect for land, they were wise enough to recognize this as a danger likely to become worse. Hunting for a practical means of halting the loss of good soil and noting that a field of stubble or standing crop seemed to shelter exposed soil for a few rods on the downwind side, they undertook in 1917 to alternate strips of summerfallow and strips of crop, much as L. P. Tuff had done; the growing crop or stubble on one side would furnish protection for exposed land in the adjacent strip.

The Kooles had seen Charlie Noble meeting with some success by planting strips of one or two drill widths. Their method was to make the strips ten to twenty rods in width and was soon seen to be practical without being costly. A writer called it a "cornerstone in the new campaign to save soil and prevent the threat of a dustbowl."

Charlie Noble maintained constant liaison with scientists and practical people showing an interest in soil conservation and frequently conferred with the Kooles. He conceded that their plan had advantages over the one with which he had pioneered and quickly adopted their plan.

Circumstances — mainly in soil drifting — made 1920 a turning point in prairie farm practice. It became evident that only those growers who were prepared to change their methods of soil management would succeed in keeping ahead of the erosion enemy. For Noble, who had been a staunch disciple of the W. H. "Dustmulch Campbell" methods embracing fine cultivation that inevitably pulverized the soil, it was doubly difficult to abandon the old ways aimed at conserving moisture and embrace the new. But he was one of the first to identify the need to change, and he remained in a position of leadership.

He had great confidence in Oswald McConkey, who was teaching agronomy at Claresholm School of Agriculture. It was a confidence that was reciprocated and from conferences among McConkey, Noble, W. H. Fairfield, and James Murray, came one of the most important directives for the farmers of southern Alberta in that period:

1. Do not pulverize the soil with discs or harrows.
2. Use such implements as rod weeders, duckfoot cultivators, and springtooth harrows that do not pulverize but leave a rough surface.
3. If the shifting area is small, a covering of manure or straw will sometimes save a whole field.
4. Reduce the extent of bare land by growing winter rye on part of the summerfallow.
5. Consider working the farm in alternate strips of fallow and crop.
6. Co-operate with your neighbors. Soil drifting can only be controlled by community action.[3]

Of the four men who conferred in the preparation of this new directive, three had university training in agriculture; the fourth, Noble, had Grade 8 standing, but as a practising farmer who was constantly in pursuit of new and better methods, he was very much a farm teacher. The point was made clear following one of those harvest days when Noble received rural and urban people as his guests at the farm. W. D. Trego was one of those present, attending as a member of the United Farmers of Alberta, representing President Henry Wise Wood. Trego was hearing Noble for the first time and was so impressed that he wrote to the press to report what he had observed and learned about the control of soil drifting. To his surprise, he had seen no land on the big farm that was suffering from erosion, something of special significance in what was being described as southern Alberta's worst year for wind damage to the land. Lavish in his praise, Trego told the reporter: "When the day was finished, I felt I had gained more good practical commonsense ideas about farming than I had ever gained in any other day of my entire life."[4]

By 1924, according to a paper prepared by Herbert Chester of the Lethbridge Experimental Station, the Monarch-Nobleford area was almost completely stripped.[5]

Nothing moves faster than a dust storm or a new and useful idea, and after winning rather general acceptance in the Monarch-Nobleford district, strip farming came to the attention of dry land farmers in distant parts. There was a growing urgency about it, especially as the ugly circumstances of the '30s seized the country.

The year 1930 was dry and dusty; 1931 was worse in most parts of the prairies. "Black blizzards" in the latter year continued into the autumn, and one of the blackest days anybody could remember was Friday, October 9, when all of southern Alberta was blanketed with clouds of dust. City traffic came close to being halted, and street lights turned on at noon made scarcely any impression. About the only farmers who were escaping the devastation of wind were those who were strip farming and those who seeded in stubble or on land that had been cultivated without loss of the stubble. It was silt from farms being cultivated by the old methods that was polluting the air and depressing the people.

Prairie farmers were challenged as never before to find some way of cultivating their fields without burying or sacrificing the ugly but precious stubble. How was it to be done? Implements like the plow buried the stubble and all other vegetable residue completely. The disc reduced the usefulness of the stubble, burying much of it. The one-way disc and duckfoot cultivator were moderately successful in leaving a big portion of the crop residue or field "trash" on the surface where it would help to break the sweep of the offending winds. Charlie Noble's rod weeders, with which he had pioneered and some of which he had made in his own blacksmith shop, were doing the best job of leaving stubble where it would help to shield the soil from the winds. Still, it was far from perfect in keeping the soil out of the air.

The same year of 1932 brought farmers from distant points to see the Monarch-Nobleford methods of erosion control. A deputation of rural people travelled from Rosetown, Saskatchewan, and returned with determination to adopt the methods. Groups from other prairie districts did the same, and before long there were strip farming associations at Limerick, Shaunavon, Aneroid, and Gull Lake in Saskatchewan and similar bodies in Alberta.

Nor was the international boundary able to contain the new Monarch-Nobleford idea for the combat of wind erosion. In July, 1932, a large group of Montana farmers and farm leaders made a tour of southern Alberta, primarily to see strip farming in operation in the district where it had originated. Before extending their studies to the federal experimental stations at Scott and Swift Current in Saskatchewan, the American visitors praised the Nobleford-Monarch progress in arresting the damage being done by drifting. The local techniques, the visitors said, were further developed than in Montana.[6] It was probably true that many farmers in the Nobleford-Monarch district had gained more experience with soil drifting than farmers elsewhere, anywhere. Having grappled studiously with the erosion enemy for more than a decade, they were in the best position to advise others confronted with similar problems.

But in spite of areas of progress on the big prairie battlefield, the dry years continued, and soil drifting was becoming more widespread until 1935 when it was seen as a national emergency. It was in this year that the government of Canada passed the Prairie Farm Rehabilitation Act — better known as the P.F.R.A. — for the purpose of employing the best conservation measures for the restoration of productivity in prairie areas devastated by drought and drifting soil.

The plan was to prove its worth and was not instituted any too soon. Perhaps Noble did not envisage a program of the scope and magnitude of P.F.R.A., but he did have something of its kind in mind for many years before it appeared on the Parliamentary Order Papers. It can be identified in a pronouncement made by him in 1920: "Above all things let us give attention principally to the mistakes which we have made and enable the Government to see that we are deserving of any assistance it is possible for them to give us."[7]

For Charles Noble, one of the best returns from those troubled years of the '30s was in new fraternal friendships that developed between himself and members of a relatively small group of men with similar feeling and concern for soil. They were scientists, experimentalists, and practical farmers. Some of them were national figures, such as William H. Fairfield, who was superintendent of the Lethbridge Experimental Station; Asael E. Palmer, assistant superintendent who became superintendent after Dr. Fairfield's retirement; Vic Mathews, superintendent at the Scott Experimental Station; L. B. Thomson, who was superintendent at Swift Current Station; Prof. Evan Hardy, who was professor of agricultural engineering at the University of Saskatchewan; Oswald McConkey, who was at Claresholm School of Agriculture and later Professor McConkey at Ontario Agricultural College; and various others who belonged to United States universities and stations.

They knew Noble as a self-trained expert, and most of them were wise enough to listen to him. Dr. Fairfield said that he and members of his staff liked to see Noble come to the experimental station because he was one of the station's best informed visitors, always "bringing more in ideas than he took away."

In the words of Hon. Duncan Marshall: "He always believed there were better methods of dealing with drought and soil drifting than we knew of, and he pursued every avenue of information and experience that opened to him."[8]

18
THE NOBLE BLADE

In the patient search for better ways of saving prairie farms against soil drifting, Noble and his neighbors displayed the kind of determination that a coach hopes to find in the players on his football team. Resourcefulness and the will to win qualified them to be counted among the leaders in soil conservation on the continent, and 170 of them meeting at Nobleford in March, 1932, for the express purpose of improving their methods in soil management, heard A. E. Palmer of the dominion experimental station at Lethbridge — later its superintendent — sounding their praise and attributing the Nobleford-Monarch successes to ingenuity and enterprise.[1]

Leonard Koole stood at that meeting and told how strip farming had gone far toward eliminating soil drifting on his farm. The report should have brought cheers, but as everybody knew, the soils in most prairie districts were suffering more than ever from erosion and it was no time to relax. The hated "black blizzards" were more numerous in 1934 than in 1933 or any other previous year. Spring and summer were dry, and every gust of wind seemed to find soil, somewhere, that was ready to lift.

The month of May was especially bad, and many residents of Lethbridge and surrounding farms rarely went outside without goggles to protect their eyes from dust and gauze masks to keep the same silt out of their nostrils and lungs. Even homes failed to give complete protection from the obnoxious dust which sifted inside through crevices around doors and windows and other invisible cracks to settle on furniture, windowsills, kitchen utensils, and bedclothes. Homemakers setting tables for meals made it a rule to place cups and saucers and plates upside down until the moment of use.

Some of the airborne soil from prairie fields did not come to rest before travelling hundreds of miles. A news report from Chicago declared that much of the estimated twelve million pounds of dust settling daily on that city was from western Canada although nobody could be sure about the proportion of the offending dust coming from Saskatchewan and Alberta and the amounts coming from Montana and the Dakotas.[2] Some of the dust appearing over Chicago was believed to remain in the wind to end its long journey in the Ohio Valley. In any case, field dust in the eastern regions was thick enough to interrupt plane service between Chicago and St. Paul and account for certain automobile collisions where visibility was affected.

Field soil in the air was serious, and it would have been easy for prairie farmers to surrender their sense of humor. To their credit, however, most of them continued to see something — even in the dust storms — about which to chuckle. Noble would tell that on days when dust cut off the rays of the sun, his hens were seen retiring to their roosts at noon. And residents of a nearby district that happened to be in the path of a rain shower while a severe May dust storm was in progress, reported that the much needed moisture fell in the form of mud drops rather than raindrops. But in a dry spell, even a shower of mud could be greeted with a welcome.

Reflecting upon the circumstances of the year, an editor said what should have been obvious, that there was still much to learn about soil drifting. Another conference was held at Lethbridge on December 13, 1934, this one bringing together a small group of specialists who by research and study were making recognized contributions to the better understanding of soils and soil problems. Most of those attending were men with university training in science, but not all; Charlie Noble was present by invitation, not for academic reasons but because of his unsurpassed practical knowledge of soils and his dedication to their care.

Most of those in attendance at the Lethbridge meetings agreed that strip farming was likely to be the prairie farmer's first line of defense against the ravages of wind. Noble, generally a step or two ahead of most public workers, did not question this point — but he did not see it as the complete and perfect solution to the problem. He had found it definitely beneficial, but with a shift in the direction of the wind, the strips could become temporarily useless and their adoption was often seen as an added invitation to sawflies. Moreover, the strips posed an inconvenience similar to that presented by small fields on all big farms.

By all means, employ strip farming until something more effective has been proven, Noble was cautioning, adding that farmers and scientists, working together and separately, would find better methods.

There was never any conflict between the soil scientists and farmers; on the contrary, there was the best of cooperation between the groups, and the farmers were the first to proclaim the benefits accruing from the work of soil scientists at western universities and experimental farms. The soil surveys and then the new problems introduced by the dry and dusty '30s brought bigger appropriations and more people into soil studies.

Nevertheless, up to this time, it was the unpretentious and comparatively silent people on prairie farms who discovered or stumbled upon the best of the new techniques like strip farming, plowless summerfallow, and stubble mulching. Hadn't strip farming originated right there in the Monarch and Nobleford communities, and didn't plowless summerfallow begin on the farm of Rufus Bohannon at Sibbald, Alberta? The Bohannon discovery was in 1918 and many farmers were horrified. Any attempt to summerfallow without plowing seemed almost like heresy. For generations the plow was the symbol of farming. Good plowing was good farming; good farming was good plowing. But Bohannon, hoping to effect operational economies and at the same time create safeguards against soil drifting, made bold to do his summerfallowing exclusively with the duckfoot cultivator and harrows. The surface of his fields looked messy and terrible, but the yields were equal to those from land summerfallowed in the conventional way and Bohannon had less soil drifting.

The Lethbridge Experimental Station gave Bohannon's plowless summerfallows a place in its testing program, and at about the same time, 1928, Charles Noble and his neighbor Neil Withage were adopting the idea and incorporating it into their strip farming plan. The result was a further check on soil drifting, making it ever clearer that the most important single factor in these newer cultural methods was the straw or stubble component. It represented another advance toward the goal of the stubble mulch or trash cover, and again, the original use of straw or stubble was probably far back on the farm of some prairie operator beset with soil drifting and not sure how to deal with it. Seeing the soil starting to move from a knoll and, perhaps, realizing that by arresting a "blow" where it was beginning — like extinguishing a forest fire before it became a conflagration — he would choose to act promptly. But what could he do? Almost instinctively, he would haul a few stoneboat loads of barnyard manure or rotted straw from an old stack butt and spread the material on the spots where drifting was starting. Some cases of what might have been large scale erosion were checked in this way.

Noting the effect of spreading manure or straw on fields showing susceptibility to drifting, workers at the experimental station at Scott, Saskatchewan, began a series of tests with straw as a simple soil drifting preventive. They were encouraged, and one way or another, the long despised crop refuse which was so often burned in the fields gained new interest and respectability.

A. E. Palmer of the Lethbridge station was now observing that fields from which the crop stubble had been destroyed by burning drifted badly — much worse than on adjacent fields which retained their stubble on the surface. Stubble was commanding added attention, both academic and practical. If straw spread on fields could blunt the force of the winds, why not make better use of the stubble already present on the fields? One reason for failure to make better use of straw and stubble as surface dressings — especially where the straw left on the fields was heavy or the combine stubble was long — was the lack of a cultivating machine that would work the land without becoming hopelessly plugged by the great volumes of loose vegetable matter. The cultivator of needed design simply did not exist.

Noble was one of the first to sense the benefits from what was to become known as the stubble mulch or trash cover and talk about them. While still encouraging the adoption of strip farming, he was searching for the as yet undiscovered technique which would make it possible to cultivate for the destruction of weeds without destroying or burying the stubble and other vegetable residue from the previous crop. It would be unsightly to leave the field's surface strewn with leftovers — like picnic garbage in a park — but saving soil was vastly more important than the housecleaned appearance of a farm field.

Nobody knew better than Noble that the best use of stubble and straw was waiting for changes in cultivating implements. As early as 1921, he told C. W. Peterson, editor of the *Farm and Ranch Review*, that the growing menace of wind erosion would make it necessary to find new methods of combat and revise the commonly accepted list of cultivating machines. If the increasing degree of pulverization in prairie soils was to be prevented and if stubble was to be used to gain the maximum in soil protection, farmers would be obliged to change their methods and abandon some of their time-honored cultivating implements.

"In cultivating to destroy weeds," he said at the time, "it is important to work the land with tools that will not pulverize it and endanger blowing. For this, the rod weeder is unexcelled; the duckfoot cultivator is good; the disc is dangerous and the harrow should be avoided. Give the dust mulch a wide berth."[3]

Now, a decade or more later, while individual successes were attending farm efforts around Nobleford and Monarch, the unpleasant fact remained that the soil drifting situation on the broad prairie farm front was worse, very much worse. Total precipitation at Lethbridge was down to 12.3 inches in 1930 and 11.4 inches in 1931. Aggravated by dry weather and faulty methods of cultivation, the area of soil drifting had grown like the ground covered by rising flood water until scarcely a farm between Brandon and Calgary escaped completely. The cost in terms of soil resources and productivity was beyond calculation.

Whatever was being done to arrest the loss of soil, Noble told delegates to the December meeting of soil specialists in 1934, it was not enough. An immediate need, he hastened to say, was for implements designed to permit summerfallowing under a heavy covering of stubble and other trash without burying that blanket. Existing cultivators lacked clearance and became clogged with the vegetable material. He could tell about his attempts to reconstruct the duckfoot cultivators with additional clearance by arranging the shovels in three rows instead of two, thereby spacing them farther apart in each row — but still the cultivator collected straw and stubble and plugged. It was easier to talk about it, the speaker warned, than to find the solution, but something had to be done by the machine companies or the farmers themselves.

Noble made no claim to being an inventor, but as with many of the men who came to the homestead country, frontier necessity awakened latent resourcefulness. An early settler at Melfort, unable to obtain replacements for his buggy wheels with spokes, made one solid wooden wheel after another until his buggy was rolling over the trails with what the neighbors identified as "the shiplap rattle." When Charlie Thomas, one of the original Barr Colonists at Lloydminster, broke the bolt of his precious gun, he knew that his only hope of obtaining a replacement was in making one. With a railroad spike and an improvised forge, he heated and pounded and fitted the metal piece until it took the shape of the intricate gun bolt and found that it worked. And when Tom Sukanen, who homesteaded near Macrorie, Saskatchewan, wanted a phonograph, he made one, and when he needed new clothes, he began by making a knitting machine.

As the records proved, the Nobles had propensities for inventiveness. Charlie's brother Newell James, one-time secretary-treasurer of the Noble Foundation, Limited, used his spare time in 1920 and '21 to produce a dustless threshing machine. Based on a revolutionary principle, it would have depended upon fans instead of the traditional cylinder with concaves. The inventor — like all inventors — was filled with confidence about the machine's future and formed a company to produce models and market the manufacturing rights. Even in 1925, shareholders in and around Lethbridge were sure one of the big manufacturing companies would want the patent and their fortunes would be assured.

To list the inventions for which Charlie Noble could take the credit would be a convincing exercise. The full account is probably not known, but the list would have to include the famous cable car by which thousands of bushels of grain grown on the Cameron Ranch farm were moved across the Old Man River to be delivered by horse-drawn wagons at Chin, reducing the total delivery distance by more than half what it would have been otherwise. Then successively among the Charlie Noble inventions of agricultural importance were the self-unloading bundle racks employed to keep the big threshing separators working to capacity and the big team hitches which increased the man-hour efficiency of hired horsemen. It seems that he was the first or one of the first, to suggest double disc cultivation, using an in-throw disc and an out-throw disc in unison and recommending manufacture to the Bissell Company.[4] The double disc proved invaluable in cultivating new breaking, and the Noble-designed seed drills with high clearance for planting on trash covered land and widely spaced seed rows for dry farming conditions were immediately and permanently useful. But it was the Noble Blade Cultivator that found the most crucial role in arresting the peril of soil drifting on the Canadian plains and even in the western parts of the United States. It was also the invention that brought its maker the greatest satisfaction and international fame.

It took a trip to California to set the stage for the drama of the blade. Normally, Noble gave no thought to holidays. Busy people, he reasoned, didn't have time for them, and those who found satisfaction in their work didn't need them. He changed the pace of his activities on Sundays and went to church, but even there he found it difficult to detach himself from his weekday work and problems and plans. Friends and members of his family wished he would take a holiday, get away for a spell of relaxation, especially after the dry and discouraging summer of 1935, and they prevailed upon him to visit California.

They reminded him that he was sixty-two years of age and should be learning how to "take it easy." Their intentions were of the best, but as advisers, they were wasting their wind. In California, his days began at the customary rising hour of 5 a.m. and were packed with activity, as they would have been back in Alberta. He could not forget the woes of drought, depression, and drifting soil on his prairies and was obsessed with the desire to do something to ease the multiple burden.

Californians and other Americans, Noble soon discovered, were scarcely less conscious of the dangers. Their first question for a Canadian visitor at that time was for the health of the Dionne quintuplets born at Callandar, Ontario, in the previous year, and their second concerned the extent of drought and soil losses on the Canadian side. As usual, the American authorities had done a better job in ascertaining the extent of soil losses, and the statistics were most alarming.

It was being reported that areas laid waste by erosion in the United States had reached a total of 52,465,097 acres, and Noble was being asked if the Canadian position relative to acreage under cultivation was better or worse. The Americans were, quite properly, taking a serious view of their losses, and one of their leaders was saying that if current conditions continued, the American people, "as a nation, had less than 100 years to go; we are in the position of an individual far gone in tuberculosis or cancer."[5]

Noble's fears were reinforced rather than relieved. He could not get it out of his mind that better farming with better tools offered the best hope in those troubled times in both Canada and the western parts of the United States. He had the feeling that the vast North American prairie region affected by wind erosion was waiting for a new type of cultivator that would cut deeply enough to destroy the weeds without disturbing the rooted stubble standing as if to guard the soil which was its parent. If the machine companies would not or could not produce such an implement, Charlie Noble would not rest until he himself had made an attempt, at least.

While still dreaming about that cultivator of new type, Noble happened to see a California farmer using a straight blade tool to cut into the subsoil to loosen his sugar beets as an aid in lifting them. The blade was heaving the soil and disturbing weeds without making much change in the general appearance of the field. At once he caught a visionary glimpse of something similar performing cultivation duty at Nobleford and doing it without depriving the land of its surface trash and standing stubble.

Noble was instantly excited. He needed access to a blacksmith shop. Happily, he had a friend in S. C. Oertley, who had worked on the Noble farm in Alberta and was now living in California. Oertley had a shop and Noble was invited to use it.

Noble was capable of being a good blacksmith, and now, starting with an old road grader blade nine feet long, a borrowed forge and anvil, and an idea, he was in his glory. He was creating something in which he had faith. As he reshaped the highly tempered steel and fixed it by means of two stout arms to a frame, then gave it two wheels and a means of depth control, the days passed quickly. He was spending long hours at the shop, forgetting even to stop at appointed mealtimes.

The first model with straight blade was completed and put to a test in a California orange grove. It did not work perfectly, but it pleased its inventor and left him with determination to make it better. It was really one of the great moments of his life, giving him a taste of the satisfaction an artist feels at the completion of a picture or a musician knows when he has composed a new melody.

Having brought his creation to an advanced stage, Noble wanted to get back to his own shop at Nobleford to make a better model. Gripped by a boyish form of excitement, he cut short his planned stay in California, loaded the crude cultivator on a trailer, and headed for home.

The Nobleford farm shop rang again with the clank of a smithy's hammer as the chief, with the help of Niels Kristoffersen, pounded out new blades and new frames, making each model a little better than the last one. When it came time to start summerfallowing, Noble had four straight blade implements complete and ready for service. All the summerfallowing of that season was done with the four blades, and Noble was happy with the result.

Neighbors and friends came to inspect the fields and satisfy themselves that the weeds had indeed been knocked out and the stubble was still standing. Some of the visitors asked Mr. Noble if they might place orders for similar machines. Charlie Noble was always an accommodating fellow and agreed to make some additional cultivators although he had no thought at that stage of branching into the manufacturing business. The farm blacksmith shop became a busy place, and about fifty cultivators were constructed for local sale in 1937. As orders and sales increased — some coming from a distance — it was natural that the man behind the operations would be attracted by the possibility of manufacturing on a worthwhile commercial basis.

If Noble needed more encouragement, he got it in 1937, the year in which much of the prairie country was caught in the worst dust storms in human memory. June 2, 1937, was a day which residents between Regina and Calgary would never forget. The news from Medicine Hat told that: "The worst dust storm in the history of the district struck shortly before 9 p.m. A gigantic black cloud rolling in from the Northwest, plunged the city into darkness as black as night.... Furniture, floors and goods in store windows were covered with a heavy grey dust that almost completely blotted out their original coloring. Confectionary keepers rushed to cover fruit and other window goods with newspapers, rugs and anything else available. Grit filtered through windows and doors, no matter how tightly shut, covering everything with a dull-grey film. Pedestrians caught in the storm sought shelter with faces almost unrecognizable under the coating of dust.... Autoists, unable to see clearly for more than a few yards, drew to a complete standstill at the sides of streets. For an hour and a half the storm raged and indistinct lights were all that were visible across a street."[6]

The urban distress was bad enough; worse by far was the loss of soil carried from farm fields, and agricultural people noted again that some fields escaped better than others. Noble's fields seemed to have been spared, and there was renewed interest in Noble's methods and Noble's new cultivating implement.

A few weeks later, a big crowd of southern Albertans assembled at the Braehead picnic ground near Nanton to hear two featured speakers, C. S. Noble speaking on the control of soil drifting and H. J. Mather of the experimental station at Lethbridge on the Prairie Farm Rehabilitation Act. Under the headline "Noble Outlines Methods of Farming to Prevent Soil

Drifting," the news story explained that Mr. Noble was one of the first to strip farm in Alberta and then quoted him as saying: "Before drifting gets more serious, avail yourselves of every possible protection against it. It can be stopped." It was his urgent plea to prairie people and his answer to those who were saying, "It can't be stopped," and were ready to surrender to the forces of 1937. It may have been the most important message of that unhappy year.[7]

Again, he was urging plowless cultivation or stubble mulch tillage, employing methods and machines which would keep the plant trash on the surface, "leaving the moist soil down and the dry soil up." He then showed pictures of homemade cultivators, fashioned by farmers who couldn't wait for the machine companies to produce them and make them available. One of the pictures showed a four-bottom plow frame fitted with four large duckfoot shovels, constructed in a farm shop at Barons, that had served the search for better cultural methods in a truly historic way, and another picture, no less historic, depicted the first grader blade mounted on a heavy frame. What the speaker, in his modesty, did not explain was that both machines seen in pictures were of his own designing, the latter being the forerunner of the new Noble blade which was at that moment winning attention wherever men were engaged in combating soil drifting.

In the next year, 1938, Charles Noble made and sold more than fifty of the blade cultivators, with nineteen of them being sold to the United States Soil Conservation Service and several to Canadian experimental stations for testing. It brought special satisfaction to him when the famous team of soil scientists F. L. Duley and J. C. Russell, working at University of Nebraska, became interested in the blade and acquired the machines needed for study and testing. The Duley and Russell interest did more; it marked the beginning of a long and mutually beneficial association between Noble and the two celebrated scientists. Noble took opportunity on various occasions to visit the two men at Lincoln, Nebraska, and they, in turn, found Noble to be a source of great help and called upon him quite frequently.

With the benefit of experience, certain changes came to the Noble blade. Gradually, the straight bar was replaced by a V-shaped blade, but the effect was about the same, undercutting weeds and leaving stubble on the surface to blunt the force of wind and to catch and hold snow. Writing authoritatively in 1952, Shirley F. Noble explained that the straight blade was still popular for deep tillage but that the V-type was in more general use and was being made in two shapes: "For light sandy soil there is the pointed 75-degree V-blade, and for reasonably firm soil, the wide-angled 100-degree V-blade."[8]

Blade manufacture was carried on by blacksmith shop methods for a few years, but as sales mounted, it demanded bigger and more pretentious facilities. A factory worthy of the name was built in 1941, and about 125 cultivators were made and sold in 1942, then 200 in 1943. Wartime restrictions on metal materials became deterrents to production, but at war's end, factory output jumped to almost a thousand cultivators in 1946. A still bigger plant was needed and there, in the village of Nobleford — one of the most unlikely places in Canada for an implement factory — the new structure was under construction in 1951. In its first three years, the new plant turned out about a million dollars' worth of Noble cultivators, with more than half of the new units going to fill orders from United States purchasers, mainly in the states of Washington, California, Oregon, Kansas, Texas, Montana, Idaho, Utah, and Oklahoma. A few blades went overseas to points as remote as Egypt and South Africa.

For Mr. Noble, the promotion of his cultivator was like a new and exciting career, and he seized the opportunity of combining cultivator publicity with soil care evangelism. As son Shirley wrote: "He travelled extensively, calling on farmers, Experimental Stations and soil conservation personnel, often with a blade implement in tow behind his car, and speaking at farmers' meetings as far south as the Texas Panhandle. Noble Farms Ltd., was changed to Noble Cultivators Ltd. and was confined exclusively to the manufacturing business."[9]

By 1955, the unique prairie factory was employing seventy people, representing a big part of the Nobleford population, and the mechanical output was being extended and varied to include the Noble hoe drills with clearance for combine straw and stubble.

Perhaps it would have been more profitable to have located such a factory at Calgary or Winnipeg or Lethbridge, and Noble was often asked why he had selected the small community. His smile betrayed the reason; it was largely sentiment. The plant could furnish jobs for friends and neighbors and help to keep young fellows in the district. After all, it was the village of which he was the founding father, its first mayor, and its planner. He could recite the village's history and recall the efforts to make Nobleford a beautiful and good place to live. He could enjoy telling about long-outdated bylaws — like No. 22 that stated: "No motor vehicle shall be operated on any street at a greater speed than one mile in four minutes." It meant, in effect, that any moderately fast buggy horse could pass the local automobiles travelling at the upper limit of allowable speed.

Noble Cultivators Ltd. experienced triumphs and the usual reverses. One of the honors which would have warmed the heart of the founder was the Industrial Achievement Award for 1973, presented by the Pacific Northwest Region of the American Society of Agricultural Engineers. It was the first time that an Alberta plant had qualified for the honor, and the presentation gave occasion for a review of the remarkable thirty-seven-year rise from a humble blacksmith shop operation in 1936 to a modern 50,000 square foot factory using 4,000 tons of steel a year, employing one hundred workers, turning out cultivators, chisel plows, distinctive hoe drills, packers, harrows, and other implements, listing 600 dealers in western Canada and seventeen western States of the Union, and sending sixty percent of the finished goods to foreign countries. Most of the export shipments were going to the United States, as might have been expected, but some machines were being sent to other countries — Russia, Pakistan, India, Egypt, Iraq, and El Salvador. Sales were up to the range of three and four million dollars a year.

The big operation which remained as a family enterprise until sold in 1978 lived on as a monument to its founder, who, in the words of Leonard Nesbitt, possessed a rare degree of originality and an enviable "spark of genius."[10] It was a monument to pioneer struggles and unyielding determination.

19
ANIMAL HUSBANDMAN

Charlie Noble was versatile enough to qualify as the district handyman, that famous fellow who was able to break the neighbors' colts, grind valves, witch wells, repair harness, lace belts, and stick pigs. There was, however, one important difference: The handyman was commonly an extrovert who was not very successful in working for himself and had plenty of time to seek the plaudits of his friends, while Noble was so busy at directing the affairs of his farm empire that even simple household repairs sometimes waited for attention, like the kitchen table that allegedly wobbled on its legs for ten years.

The Noble versatility was on a high and an ambitious plane. An editor would pronounce him as the most imaginative farmer on the prairies, and Hon. Duncan Marshall, paying tribute to the same gift of ingenuity, said he was "the best tiller of the soil in semiarid districts."

Although Noble's special passion was for soil and soil conservation, his magic touch was most evident in crop production. At the same time, he might have rated as a leading mixed farmer had he wanted — but his involvement with horses, mules, cattle, and pigs was overshadowed by that exceptional sense of stewardship for the soil. Still, neighbors and hired helpers were quick to describe him as an outstanding horseman and a very good cattleman.

Andy Sherman, who worked for him through many years, remembered occasions when a "green" team of horses and an inexperienced driver were not getting along very well and the chief would step in and take the reins until the horses had a better idea of what was expected of them and the hired man had a better idea of handling unsettled horses. Noble's touch was that of a master horseman.

Like most farmers of his time, Noble had a special feeling of affection for horses, but he differed from most of his contemporaries by having a pronounced faith in mules, which he believed were better workers than horses. His respect for mules was like his esteem for all faithful workers. It was difficult for him to understand why Canadian farmers had treated mules like "second class citizens of the barnyard."

In their personalities, mules were as distinctive as their long ears and unemotional appearance in a horse pasture. With a sort of no-nonsense attitude, they would often ignore situations that worried the horses. Their display of indifference toward surroundings did nothing to aid an understanding of what seemed like a droll sense of humor. They liked to find ways that would force the horses with which they were hitched to carry a disproportionate share of the load. They would let the loaded wagons to which they were hitched become stuck in the mud when on an outward journey or being driven away from home stables, but never when returning and approaching the destination that held feed and water and rest, especially if it were close to the noon hour or quitting time at night. It was well known that a mule was better able to take care of itself than a horse would do. When a horse found an open door to a grain bin, it would invariably overeat and pay dearly for its excesses with colic. Not so a mule, Noble noted many times; it was wise enough to stop eating before it became the victim of gluttony. And displaying the same superior wisdom, the mule that accidentally got its foot caught in barbed wire would remain motionless and calm until released, while the horse caught in similar circumstances would become excited and add needlessly to its troubles and injury.

Sure, Noble liked mules. In 1911, he bought one of the best Spanish jacks available in the southern States and brought it to Grand View Farm where many carefully selected mares were assembled for breeding purposes. The first crop of 1912 consisting of twenty hybrid foals brought public interest and a decision on Noble's part to specialize in mule production. By 1913, every sound mare in Noble's possession was being bred to give him a mule foal.[1] In 1914, the baby mules seemed to be everywhere at Grand View.

Mules did not win the acceptance that Noble anticipated for them. Even most settlers from the United States lost interest, and breeding dwindled in the West as a whole. Nevertheless, the mules of the homestead years did perform their share of heavy farm work and deserved to be remembered. Even after disappearing elsewhere, mules remained prominently on the Noble farms, especially on the Cameron Ranch farm where one of the five main divisions or camps was stocked exclusively with mules as work animals. Station Number Two hitched only mules, partly, no doubt, because camp foreman Allendor and the general foreman for the entire Cameron Ranch, Fred Keinbaum, shared the chief's enthusiasm for mules. But with most workmen, the mules were less popular than the horses and this proved to be a handicap. "The mules were too smart for the men," Robert Gratz explained it.

Noble was never a person to waste much time at storytelling, but he had a few favorite jokes about mules which betrayed his fondness for the animals and which he related with obvious enjoyment. One of them concerned a self-appointed weather authority he knew during his homestead years at Knox, in North Dakota. After gaining a considerable reputation for accuracy in predicting weather conditions, the fellow was pressed to reveal the secret of his successful prognostications. No weatherman would choose to divulge his trade secrets, but this one yielded to the public pressures and confessed that he was not a weather prophet at all; the real prophet was his old mule which had the talent to communicate with its owner as well as judge next week's weather. The said mule, it was told, had even prophesied the election in 1896 of William McKinley to become the twenty-fifth president of the United States and revealed his majority correctly. Such a mule, certainly, should have been taken to Washington and kept there to advise the president. In any case, it was a mule triumph and Noble enjoyed it.

Acquaintances who were amused at Noble's sentiment for mules should not have been surprised at his interest in pigs and his large scale involvement with them. Perhaps he thought like Sir Winston Churchill, who was reported to have said that he admired dogs for their friendliness and loyalty, cats for their self-reliance, but pigs were his favorites because of the forthright way they looked him straight in the eye and met him as equals.

The big adventure in pigs resulted in part at least from Noble's sense of patriotic duty. Just as his extensive wheat farms of 1917 and 1918 were in response to the national plea for more cereal grains to meet wartime needs at home and abroad, so it was during the years of World War II that Noble heard the national call to produce more bacon for Britain. The campaign conducted by governments of the time made the need very urgent and very clear.

Increasing pork production during those war years when many young farmers were in uniform or working in war industry was not easy, but ingenious people found ways of adding the responsibility of caring for pigs to their existing lists of chores. Nor were farmers alone in their adoption of wartime pigs. With the fervor of patriotism, many professional and other urban people bought bred sows and placed them with farmers, promising to perform all the essential chores of feeding and cleaning the animals — and, of course, taking all the profit or loss from the enterprise.

It became fashionable as well as patriotic and profitable to be involved actively with pigs. School teachers with pigs to feed felt they could decently leave classrooms promptly or a few minutes early for the drive to the country. Businessmen advanced their closing hours by a few minutes or half an hour because they had feedhoppers to fill and water to carry at the end of their drive to nearby farms. For some of them, it was a new and refreshing experience to be engaged in the business of producing something as basic as human food.

There was ample grain feed for pigs — barley, oats, wheat, rye, and byproducts — and market prices looked attractive to farmers who had only recently emerged from the long years of drought and ruinous prices. It was easy to be patriotic when dollar returns were high, but not so easy when helpers were extremely scarce. In any case, thousands of Canadians who confessed to knowing nothing about pigs undertook to produce the animals which would furnish the much discussed Wiltshire sides. Before the end of the war, every adult seemed to be on familiar terms with Wiltshire sides, understanding thoroughly that a Wiltshire was a trimmed side weighing about sixty pounds, given a mild brine cure, and wrapped for export to Britain.

Charlie Noble heard the call to employ bacon-type pigs to serve the country and serve himself, and in answering it, as his friends would have expected, he did it in his typically giant way. Because of continuous and destructive rains in the previous autumn, Noble found himself with large quantities of tough and damp grains, particularly difficult to market. Moist grain, however, was still a good feed for pigs, provided, of course, it was fed before it had time to heat or spoil in the warm spring weather.

If the idea of employing pigs to market unsalable grains was a good one, it would still be good when tried on a large scale, Charlie Noble would reason. His plan, as might have been expected, was for the biggest pig raising operation the south country had seen. It would be at Grand View Farm on Nobleford's east side, and Mr. Noble in 1942 engaged Ray and Wilma Flitton, newlyweds, to live on the premises and take charge of the enterprise at a combined salary of $130 per month and their board. Ray Flitton, who was raised at Claresholm, was familiar with pig production, and Mrs. Flitton, with a Japanese girl to help her, was ready to assume the responsibility for running the big Grand View house with its ten-foot ceilings, preparing meals for as many as twenty-eight workmen, looking after the beds and bedding for a similar number of farm employees, and caring for the farm garden. Baking seventy-five loaves of bread a week and washing the linen from twenty-eight beds were just parts of the routine household chores.

Mrs. Flitton did not forget the big appetites. The young men raised in Japanese communities with only a little meat in their diets now "discovered a taste for pork chops and surprised even themselves at the quantities of their intake." It took a carcass of home-grown pork every week or two to feed the men on the farm.

Finding the necessary help with which to handle the thousands of pigs at that time of war stringency would have presented serious problems if Mr. Noble had not been successful in obtaining thirteen Japanese and Japanese-Canadians moved recently under war measures policies from the Pacific coast. They proved to be excellent workers, and their first assignment at Grand View Farm was in building a pig farrowing barn with twenty pens and making scores of A-shaped colony houses, each of a size to accommodate one sow and her litter to the time of weaning.

The most modern machinery for grinding and mixing feeds was installed, and one of the Japanese-Canadian employees was placed in charge to give his full time to feed preparation. Then, as soon as fences and shelters were ready, the word went out that Mr. Noble was buying sows for breeding, any breed, any color, any number, pregnant, or not yet pregnant. As Mrs. Flitton recalled, the sows began to arrive early one morning, generally by truck, and numbers increased like those of pigs being delivered at a stockyard. A score of sows came the first day, and before long the delivery total stood at 100 and finally 500.

James Murray referring to Mr. Noble wrote to say: "You will probably recall his flier in pigs in the thirties. I was at his place once when he had around 600 sows and little pigs in proportion. He was trying to eat up the wheat surplus."[2]

Spectators were surprised — all except those who understood the way the Charles Noble mind worked. Just as he had created Canada's biggest wheat-growing farm during the years of the First World War, he was now in a position to support the needs of the Second World War with the biggest pig farm.

While leaving the day-to-day problems in mass production to Ray Flitton and helpers, the chief watched attentively and saw to it that rations were scientifically compounded and pigs were receiving ample allowances of barley, wheat, tankage, fish meal, alfalfa, and mixed mineral supplements. But with such a concentration of pig numbers, it was extremely difficult to maintain good health, and pre-weaning losses were sometimes heavy.[3]

Most litters were born in the spring, but others, to the limit of facilites, were farrowed in the fall and winter.

Although the original brood sows were of various breeds and colors, only Yorkshire and Tamworth boars of the best bacon type and quality were brought in for breeding, and most of the pigs that ultimately reached market were worthy candidates for Wiltshire sides and brought enough quality to please the discriminating English consumers.

When enough pigs reached a weight between 200 and 220 pounds and were thus ready for rail shipment to the stockyard market at Lethbridge or Winnipeg, Ray Flitton and some of his helpers, believing it was easier to drive the pigs for a mile or so to the loading pens at Nobleford than to load them and haul them, would undertake the tricky task of herding the hundred or more over the route. If the animals allowed themselves to be driven quietly, the herd would be penned and ready for loading at the railway chutes an hour after leaving the farm; but pigs were not known to be very cooperative, and if each of a hundred pigs chose to race away in a different direction, the visitors who came to see a pig drive could retire with the knowledge that they had seen the première of a swine circus.

Pig raising on the mass production scale lasted at Grand View until after the end of the war. Grain markets improved, and European supplies returned to furnish bacon for Britain. Some of the Japanese-Canadians who had been employed by Mr. Noble settled permanently in southern Alberta, and one of the choreboys, George Okeita, remained in service on the Noble farms and became one of the foremen. And the Flittons left Grand View to settle on and operate their own farm near Vulcan.

Because Charlie Noble's gigantic cropping activities dwarfed everything else, including his involvement with cattle, the real scope of his mixed farming was often underestimated. The fact was that Noble kept cattle continuously and advised fellow farmers to keep them, either dairy cattle or beef cattle.

The Noble Foundation of earlier years had its own registered cattle brand, NC, on the left shoulder.[4]

Wilma Flitton recalled that even during the years of World War II, when Grand View Farm was the scene of pork production on a great scale, cows were being milked and cream was being shipped and sold. It was totally consistent with the advice that Noble had often given to younger farmers, to practise a degree of diversification or mixed farming that would insure enough revenue from the sale of animal products to pay for the groceries and clothing needed by members of the farm family.

It was not to be overlooked that Noble had a long experience in the operation of cattle feed lots. The news of 1934 told of his feed lot from which he was shipping beef cattle to Britain and giving expression to advocacy of "more livestock on the farms."

"This week," according to the news, "Mr. Noble shipped through the Southern Alberta Co-operative Association, a nice bunch of Red Label beef to the Old Country. Last fall Mr. Noble bought these cattle for his feedlot at Nobleford and he brought them to a splendid finish. Mr. Noble has been a careful student of the farm situation for years and in urging a balanced agriculture is backing his position by placing more livestock on the farms."[5]

To make the cattle shipment to England still more noteworthy, it was 1934 when circumstances of drought and depression were stifling most prairie enterprises, certainly including cattle feeding.

Noble held to his views, and at the age of eighty-three years in 1957, when Canada was facing heavy grain surplus and carry-over at the end of the crop year, he was enlarging his feed lots at Nobleford and getting ready to fatten 900 head of cattle for the spring market. It was not a new adventure but rather an old adventure on a new and bigger scale.

There were bigger feed lot operations both before and after, but none to that time were more progressive and none were under the supervision of a man of his unyielding years. Moreover, this big and fully mechanized enterprise was a farm feed lot more than a commercial unit. Making it different and strictly in keeping with mixed farming principles, Mr. Noble and his sons, Shirley and Gerald — in it together — were drawing almost exclusively upon home-grown feeds. Surplus and low grade wheat, oats, and barley were hard to sell, but close to 100,000 bushels were fed to and marketed through the Noble feed lot herds in one year. And a big part of the roughage was fed in the form of cereal silage cut before reaching maturity while the food value was high and the weeds growing in the crops could be arrested before their seeds became viable. Thus crop and weeds together were translated to useful and highly palatable cattle feed.

The forage from 400 acres of immature or damaged crop was thus recovered for silage in 1957, making for a conversion from mediocre crop to first class silage and first class beef. And as a further mark of efficient mixed farming practice, the thousands of loads of animal manure from the feed lots were hauled back to the Noble crop land to help to hold the good farmer's line against erosion and depletion. The aging chief told a reporter that the manure being spread on the fields was one of the important dividends from a feed lot.

It was the big and efficient feed lot enterprise that led Joe Balla of the *Lethbridge Herald* to make some significant observations about the man behind it. Writing in December, 1956 — less than two years before Dr. Noble's death — the newsman said: "Dr. C. S. Noble, the great farmer-industrialist who has carved one of the richest niches in Western Canada's agricultural history, hasn't come about his reputation just by chance — he has earned every bit of it. It's just as well for thousands of farmers throughout the world that he has acquired the reputation of never being quite satisfied."[6]

20
AFTER FIFTY YEARS

Fifty years and fifty harvests had passed since Charles Noble ventured into the Canadian Northwest — as eager as an orphan lamb — and decided that this was where he wanted to live and farm and die. The growing influence of his Canadian-born sweetheart in North Dakota may have had something to do with the decisions that made him a Canadian citizen from the earliest date available to him.

There were good years and poor years in that sweep of half a century — more of the former than the latter — and all profitable in experience. It was his determined view that mistakes and misfortunes can be and should be turned to good use. His record seemed to confirm it.

He had one of his best crops in 1951, and, now, the crop of 1952 gave prospect of being a better one. The West was experiencing its first uranium-staking rush and more people than ever before were searching for oil and natural gas, but Noble was glad he had remained with farming on the Canadian plains. Complementing his farming was his expanding business in manufacturing and selling blade cultivators and other lines of machinery. The manufacturing enterprise, which began in a commercial way in 1937 with the making of fifty Noble Blade Cultivators of his own designing, had grown to total plant sales of $728,000 in the most recent year, 1951, and was destined to rise to about $2,000,000 in 1967 and more than $7,000,000 in 1978.

Although this year of 1952 found him worried about his wife's health and quietly concerned about a deterioration in his own, he was trigger ready to declare that he had much for which to be thankful. He acknowledged the good fortune of his life's adventures, all of which had taught him something.

How would he like to do it all over again, starting with the homestead in North Dakota and then a Canadian homestead at Claresholm? His smile gave proof that the question was not entirely new to him and generated pleasant thoughts. And then, as if the suggestion of his fifty-year record of farming on the Canadian plains awakened fresh sentiment for the pioneer years, he confessed that he would like to travel back for a glimpse of the homestead at Knox and then return to see the homestead quarter at Claresholm, perhaps for the last time.

He had travelled back to the United States scores of times, generally to inspect the work of American experimental stations or visit big farms like that of Tom Campbell, but he had never taken time to see his first homestead since he sold it almost fifty years earlier. Son Shirley, sensing his father's sentimental interest, enquired how he would like to slip away while still thinking about the North Dakota homestead and see it as it appeared in 1952. Ah, he would like it, and Shirley was quick to volunteer to accompany as his father's driver.

"After we've seen the homestead at Knox," the young man said, "I'll drive you back to Claresholm to see what it will do for your memory. You've never talked much about homesteading at either place."

Pioneer Charles Noble was at once enthusiastic. It was agreed that the trip should not be made in haste although members of the family wondered if father and husband could really do anything leisurely. As it turned out, father and son took three weeks in making the sentimental journey to North Dakota, and the older man reminisced as he had never done in his son's presence before. Shirley Noble listened with the attention a father's recollections deserved.

It was early July when father and son drove south and crossed into Montana at Coutts. Mr. Noble's inclination was to drive by way of the Tom Campbell farm at Hardin. There Campbell had been renting 90,000 acres on the Crow Reservation. These holdings on the banks of the Big Horn River, along with some 50,000 acres in North Carolina, made him the operator of the biggest farm in the world.

As a renter rather than a landowner, Campbell's manner of farming differed greatly from Charles Noble's. His acknowledged motive was profit, and he was one of the first to mechanize. By 1930 he did not own a single workhorse. He was one of the first big farmers to mechanize completely. Differences in motives notwithstanding, Campbell and Noble were close friends, and often over the years, they visited back and forth to exchange views. Shirley Noble remembered Campbell as a big man, "almost as tall as my father, and likely to be driving a beat-up old Ford car."

Campbell, like Noble, was farming land on which the annual precipitation averaged about fifteen inches, making both feel dependent upon summerfallow. He, too, had been searching for a better way of cultivating dry land and had adopted the Noble Blade Cultivators. The bonds of friendship had become strong, but with Campbell located in the far south of the state, Shirley made the decision that a visit there would take too much of the time intended for Knox. "You can't stop every time you see a Noble blade in a field, you know," the son warned.

Instead of calling upon Campbell, the Nobles stopped briefly to exchange ideas with leaders in farm research at Havre, Montana, which was not out of the way. There they received a glowing report about the results from field tests with the Noble blade, and there they were greeted by numerous people who said: "Oh, you are the Canadians who gave us one of our best tools for the battle against soil drifting."

The next stop would be unspectacular Knox, North Dakota, about which one of the nearby residents said facetiously, "Until you've seen Knox, you haven't seen the world." Of course, the town had changed greatly, and for the man who had not seen it for fifty years, the familiar landmarks and the familiar faces had vanished. Charlie Noble met a few people with familiar names — like the Delameters — but nobody he could recognize, and briefly, he wondered why he had bothered to return.

But gradually, with his memory serving him better, the Knox surroundings were assuming a friendlier form. He had not forgotten the road over which he had travelled, often on foot, from the town to the homestead, and without delay the Alberta car was turned to it. Mr. Noble was hoping that at least one of his modest buildings was still standing. In this he was disappointed, but the sight of the farm setting brought a flood of memories that inspired his speech. During the next few days, Shirley Noble was to hear more about his father's years at Knox than he had ever heard before.

They were years of heavy toil, during which the tough Dakota sod was broken with four willing horses and a walking plow whose plowshare would not stay sharp. With an extra plowshare, however, he found that by walking to the village in the evenings and carrying a share, he was able to have one moderately sharp one on the plow and another at the blacksmith's shop being sharpened. Twice a week he walked to the village with one share under his arm and then back home in the darkness with the other share.

Even in that early period, as Shirley Noble was now discovering, his father was displaying the instincts of an experimentalist. For his first homestead crop, he planted flax as well as wheat; flax was an experiment, and then he harrowed the land after the crop was above the ground. Neighbors who saw him do it, he recalled, were horrified and came to make a closer examination and see if he had really destroyed the young plants. But as the season advanced, neighborly concern ended, and in the fall, when Noble's flax gave the highest yield in the area, the neighbors came again, this time to seek Noble's advice about planting and cultivating.

Of the shack and stable he had contructed, there was now no trace. But there was the location of the well, at least a depression in the ground to positively identify the spot where in the course of digging, he had fallen down the twenty-foot hole and broken his leg. Now he could chuckle about the pain and worry he suffered as he struggled with rope and ladder to get his hurting body out of the well. Typically, he noted that it might have been worse; he "might have found himself down there without the ladder."

Recuperation was long and distressing, but now, after more than fifty years, it was being told how the unhappy victim spent his waiting time. Of course he would not be idle; he read twelve volumes on ancient history and then, after becoming somewhat more mobile, he went to Minneapolis and registered for a winter course in business and accounting. It was one more expression of a lifelong conviction that misfortunes should be turned to advantage.

But Charles Noble had not returned to these acres of other years merely to muse romantically about his fall down the well and other homestead experiences. It was becoming increasingly evident that there was another and stronger motivating desire which he could hide no longer. That chief concern, sentimental indeed, was for the soil on his old homestead farm. How had successive owners cared for that soil? Had there been the proper diligence in the control of weeds? Had fertility been reasonably maintained? How well had the operators succeeded in preventing soil drifting and other erosion on the land for which he held lingering feelings of parental kind?

To obtain answers to his questions, he lost no time in

wandering into the fields which had been broken at the agonizing rate of two acres per day by means of his walking plow. There he studied the inroads made by weeds, assessed crop stands to determine soil productivity, and searched to satisfy himself that erosion in all its evil forms had been held in check. He was visibly relieved; those to whom that homestead farm had been entrusted must have been at least moderately devoted to good soil management.

Shirley Noble watched with special interest. He understood his father better than anybody else. Often he had heard his parent declare that it was both stupid and immoral to allow soils to deteriorate needlessly. He wished that all farmers, especially his two sons, would cultivate a reverence for soil and a dislike for weeds. Shirley recalled the day in his boyhood when his father placed a garden hoe in his hands, saying, "Get busy. I want you to learn to hate weeds."

Now that Mr. Noble had satisfied himself that the soil to which he had become wedded more than fifty years before was still in good order — the real but undeclared reason for the trip — he could relax and think and talk about more frivolous events in the homestead years. He recalled his meeting with the Canadian Presbyterian minister, Rev. Simon Fraser, and then with his visiting sister who became Mrs. Noble. He remembered the day when Simon Fraser came out to the farm to help him in making hay and an irreverent field mouse climbed up the ministerial pant leg, inspiring hayfield oratory that was described as louder and more expressive than any heard from the Presbyterian pulpit at Knox.

Charlie Noble could say that he had good neighbors at Knox, mainly young men like himself, and his brother Newell James came at that time to become the school principal at nearby Rugby. But there could be no doubt that of the people he came to know in North Dakota, it was Margaret Fraser who did the most to change and shape his life. It was here that she demonstrated the Fraser thrift and enterprise he admired, and now, with Shirley driving, he was pleased to locate two landmarks in the form of cottage homes, still standing, on which he and Margaret Fraser had left the marks of their first joint venture.

As he explained the existence of the cottages to his son, it was like this: When Margaret came to visit her brother and remained to teach school at Leeds, a few miles away, she qualified for a teacher's salary of about $350 per year. After a couple of years in that position, she had most of her wages in savings and decided to make an investment. She and Charlie talked about it, and she was attracted by the idea of building a small house in Knox and renting it at a monthly rate that would furnish a worthwhile dividend. Charlie said that if Margaret's money bought the needed lumber and nails, he would spare her much of the initial expense by doing the carpentry for her. With such an economy in the building, Margaret's savings were found to be sufficient for two cottages instead of one.

Charlie Noble was already well qualified as a woodworker, and Margaret became the owner of two houses available for renting and the village of Knox benefited by two additional homes. And now, to Charlie's surprise and satisfaction, the two structures he recognized readily were standing and in good repair as if to greet him.

Father and son returned home agreeing that this sentimental journey into the past had been a good idea. It was such a good idea that they agreed to extend it as soon as possible by driving to the Claresholm homestead. It would be but a short journey, and a couple of days would allow plenty of time for both the trip and the appropriate visiting in the district where the Nobles began married life and where his business and farming interests took a new and broader shape. Actually, he had never broken his personal association with Claresholm as he had done with Knox. Moreover, it was where Shirley was born, and even for him, some faint memories survived.

The two trips were profitable, leaving son Shirley with a better understanding and appreciation of his father's notable career. When the younger man enquired how it had been achieved, he heard again what his father had said many times: "Whatever thy hand findeth to do, do it with all thy might."[1]

For the pioneer there was the satisfaction of knowledge that the soil on all the land for which he had ever assumed the responsibility of care was still productive and good. What more rewarding comfort in the life of one who believed that the conservation of soil and other natural resource gifts was the greatest moral challenge facing mankind.

For a brief spell, at least, he seemed to forget the nagging worry of his own failing health. But whether he admitted it or not at that time, he had leukemia, and leukemia was known to be merciless.

21
THE MEASURE OF THE MAN

Noble was a challenging subject for study — but not a simple one. In temperament he was as conspicuously different as the spike of wheat that gave rise to the Marquis variety, and as complex as his mules' chromosomes. Being a man of few words, people around him were often left guessing about his thoughts and aspirations. There was never any doubt concerning his dedication to soil and conservation, and for that reason alone he should have been enshrined in western memory. But many other questions remained unanswered or incompletely answered.

Why was he so determined to farm on an extraordinarily large scale, while arguing in favor of farm units of more moderate size? What was the principal motivating force in his dramatic life? Was he ambitious to be rich or famous or merely to achieve an independence his parents never knew? Did he have the muscle to be an athlete or the patience to be a public servant or the secret desire to be a scientist? Was he without more than a modicum of sentiment as some spectators allowed themselves to believe?

Most people possess at least two images, one known to the public and another that only close friends and associates are permitted to know. Generally, the latter is more reliable and meaningful than the former. Those westerners who read about Noble in the press or visited the farm on open house occasions knew him as the biggest farm operator in Canadian history, the man who would harness an earth-shaking battery of steam tractors to break sod on the Cameron property at the unprecedented rate of 400 acres a day in 1918 or the one who would thresh half a million bushels of grain in one season and do it with no more pretension than that of a man hoeing potatoes.

A few writers like C. W. Peterson, president and directing editor of the *Farm and Ranch Review,* attempted to peer under the veil of performance and relate the achievements to the man. He saw new meaning in the Noble farms where "nothing is done without careful consideration and forethought, [where] the tidy appearance of fences, buildings and yards spoke volumes. It was evident that there was a master mind behind it all . . . . It is very clear," he wrote, "that Mr. Noble is a man with a head for detail and being an indefatigable worker, has the knack of seeing things done."[1]

Not so widely known was the judgment of people who were perpetually close to Noble and worked with him. They insisted that money was not the prime objective, and if he had wanted fame and more notoriety, he could have had them. Members of the press were fascinated by this super farmer and pursued him, but while refusing to flee from reporters, he did not go out of his way to win press attention.

Speaking as one who worked for Mr. Noble and worked with him, saw him early and late, and often prepared meals and snacks for him was Mrs. Wilma Flitton. "He was gentle and kind and shy," she wrote. "He went to bed with the chickens and was up with them at 4 a.m. . . went to church every Sunday, quietly in and quietly out. He was friendly and gracious but not an easy mixer. He invited advice and then, generally, ignored it to follow his own inclinations."[2]

Mrs. Flitton recalled the times when he asked her husband, Ray, and the two Noble boys to accompany him to the fields to consider a policy for cultivation. After each had expressed an individual opinion and Mr. Noble had stated his own, he would conclude the mid-field conference by saying: "Well, it's agreed that we will do it this way," always the way he had favored and suggested at the outset.

"He didn't seem to eat much," Mrs. Flitton noted. "Maybe he had uclers; with his restless nature and unrelaxing ways, he seemed like a candidate." She remembered him coming in at mealtime or a little later, often saying: "Please give me a bowl of bread and milk; I'm in a hurry."

As those who watched him knew very well, Noble had the heart of a scientist. He was a lifelong student of Nature and a lifelong student by nature. With more education, perhaps a university degree in agriculture along with his natural ingenuity and drive, he would have been precisely the kind of man the new Prairie Farm Rehabilitation Act administration needed in 1935. Even in the absence of university training, however, he was conducting experiments that the scientists could not ignore.

Always on good terms with people at the experimental farms, there was mutual benefit. Superintendent W. H. Fairfield said he liked to see Mr. Noble coming to the Lethbridge station because "he always brought as many new ideas as he took away." The same popular farm leader, with many years in the experimental farm service, wished he could hire young fellows with as much zeal for experimentation. To be testing came instinctively to this man with an orderly and enquiring mind. Everything he did was systematized; even when travelling with his family, he made notes about new practices and inventions that came to his attention and might hold even a remote chance of being useful in his work. Articles on agricultural subjects were clipped and filed faithfully or pasted in scrapbooks. It was typical of the man that in his constant battle against weeds, all known patches of the persistent Canada thistles were marked and mapped the way submerged rocks and shoals would be identified on a navigator's chart.

He maintained communication with research workers in both western Canada and the western states, helping them almost as often as they helped him. Some of the leading soil scientists in the American Midwest admitted a debt to him. F. L. Duley, writing on behalf of the famous research team comprising J. C. Russel and himself, said appreciatively, "We have kept in touch with him for nearly 20 years . . . . Russel and I have both visited his farm and plant in Alberta. We have considered him our most reliable and active co-operator."[3]

Reporting to O. S. Longman in June, 1956, Duley noted that he had only a few days earlier written to Mr. Noble to seek his suggestions and advice concerning new research work in wind erosion control which was being started in western Nebraska. The writer made it seem like a routine letter that had been directed to his friend Charles Noble.

Most private operators of big farms thought they were too busy to indulge in experimental work on their own behalf and on their own land. Not Noble. To him it was important to know the comparative costs for plowing with horses, gasoline engines, and steam tractors on his own fields, and when he obtained the answers, he discovered to his satisfaction that a thousand other prairie farmers were eager to know his findings. He wanted to know the exact differences in crop yields and costs when land was prepared in different ways, by moldboard plows, duckfoot cultivators, and the blade cultivators of his own invention. He did not believe that he was competing with the experimental farms but, rather, complementing their more elaborate efforts.

His program of experimentation as stated by his brother Newell James was continuous for many years, and his techniques led visitors to enquire: "Where did he learn how to do it?" From 1912 or 1913, he had a moderately big field laid out in carefully measured and staked plots, looking very much like fields of test plots seen at experimental farms at Brandon or Indian Head or Lethbridge.

The 1916 tests, for example, showed plant selection work being conducted along professionally familiar lines, even to the rod rows. Some of the tests were based on single-head rows, some on prescribed numbers of individual seeds per row. Noble's notes written in that same year revealed his seed counts for certain experimental plantings, "3,418 kernels from one hundred heads of oats planted," and "3,129 kernels from one hundred heads of wheat planted." The same surprising notes indicated that by his meticulous calculations, it took 757,218 kernels of oats to plant an acre and that the total length of all the drills, six inches apart, on an acre was 1,045,440 inches. What patience was required!

Perhaps he was carrying private experimentation too far. He didn't think so. Perhaps the neighbors would say that such experimental labor was unnecessary and a waste of time when there were experimental farms established to conduct the studies. But Noble, untrained in the ways of scientific methods though he was, had some advanced concepts of research and would have enquired: "How do you know that any new information will not be useful?"

Not satisfied with the advice farmers were receiving about rates of seeding, he conducted his own tests and carried them along for some years. The rates recommended previously were, in his opinion, too high, and for the best returns under prairie conditions, his tests seemed to support his contention.

In conducting both his seed plots and private crop experiments, it is probable that Charles Noble had both the guidance and encouragement of his friend Oswald McConkey, who became instructor in field husbandry and soils at the new school of agriculture at Claresholm. Certainly the plots on

Section 11 of Grand View Farm saw more activity after McConkey came to the district. He believed that every grower should have seed plots and experimental plots. Of course he would be delighted with Noble's interest and perseverance.

There did not seem to be any reason why the same plots of one twentieth of an acre and bigger could not serve the double purpose and furnish both high grade seed and experimental information. Accordingly, six-row barley being propagated for seed was planted at six different rates — ½ bushel per acre, 1 bushel per acre, 1¼ bushels per acre, 1½ bushels per acre, 1¾ bushels per acre, and 2 bushels per acre. The same experimental plantings were paralleled with registered Marquis wheat except that there were twelve plots and seeding was at one peck, two pecks, three pecks, four pecks, five pecks, six pecks, seven pecks, eight pecks, nine pecks, ten pecks, eleven pecks, and twelve pecks per acre, respectively.

In 1919, Rosen and Common rye were included in the rate-of-seeding tests, and by 1920 both the farm seed fields and the experimental plots were being expanded. The rate-of-seeding trials were being continued, and at the same time, old and new varieties were being grown for performance tests and for observation in bigger plots, among them, Banner oats, Alaska oats, Liberty oats, hand-selected Marquis wheat, "electrically treated Marquis wheat," Quebec No. 20 corn, North Western Dent corn, Giant Russian sunflowers, Irish Cobbler potatoes, Carter's Early Favorite potatoes, and more.

The electrically treated seed, proposed by a Manitoba professor, had been catching public attention, but Noble's tests showed the untreated seed to be far more productive than the treated kind, 280 pounds of clean seed per plot from the treated stock and 496 pounds of clean seed per plot from the untreated parent seed. The result was quite sufficient to give the new and high-sounding idea the setback it no doubt deserved.

Nobody suggested that Noble's experimental program equalled or even approached that of the nearby dominion station, but for an individual farmer — and a big and busy one at that — it identified its planner and creator as a man of rare distinction. But what was clearer was that he was a man of many parts and a man of many distinctions. Somebody said he was not an athlete. Was it so? True, he had never allowed himself much time for athletics and games. Having found satisfaction and pleasure in performing useful tasks, he had never been drawn to unproductive amusement. For most of his life he was just too busy to be pitching horseshoes on summer afternoons and curling on winter evenings.

But if he failed to impress those around him with his athletic skills, it was not necessarily from lack of muscle and coordination and stamina, the essentials from which athletes are made. He could outrun most boys of his age in the years at State Centre, and, at sixty, he could still run with impressive speed when circumstances like an angry bull or a loose and wayward horse dictated the need.

The roster of Claresholm's first baseball team, playing against Nanton, Granum, and Fort Macleod in 1906 and 1907, showed Noble as the pitcher and winning an acceptable share of the games. It was serious baseball, played as though the peace and prosperity of southern Alberta communities depended upon the outcome.

One of Noble's helpers remembered a moment of noon hour leisure when some of the workers on the farm were indulging in frivolous stone throwing to see who could hit a tin can at fifty yards. The chief came along and was invited to see how close he could come to the target. To everybody's surprise, Mr. Noble stopped, picked up three or four stones, and hurled them like an old baseball professional and hit the target and then hit it a second time. The young fellows were properly impressed and slightly humiliated by the performance of "the old man."

Being tall and lean, Noble "didn't look like a weight lifter," as one of his men remarked, "but he was strong enough that no haltered horse ever got away from him." The same man mentioned the tug of war of about 1922 when the Lethbridge Board of Trade was invited for a picnic at the Noble farm. The visitors from the city challenged the men of the Noble Foundation staff to a tug of war. Naturally, the local men accepted and then persuaded the chief to be their captain and anchorman. It was the last event of the day, and the contest began with every indication that the visitors, with additional weight, would have an advantage.

The extra weight was, indeed, moving the Lethbridge men to victory when the tall anchorman, sensing hope in coordination, called "Heave," then "Heave" again. With repeated calls at evenly spaced intervals, Noble's uncoached men got the idea and little by little, the bigger city men were pulled across the finish line.

He was not deficient in athletic skills although he was often short of the time needed to express them. In the same sense, he was not lacking in sentiment but may have been short of the time needed to display it. He would never, by design, place his sentiment on parade. Next to his family, his church and his soil were the dominating forces in his life. He had a religious zeal for all of these.

The big house which was ready for occupation at the end of 1917[4] symbolized his feeling that nothing was too good for his family. And what a house! The plan was drawn in California where the Nobles went to winter in 1916, and the cost was over $30,000 at a time when such an expenditure could be expected to build a mansion. With running water from two wells, plumbing, an electric lighting plant, and an indoor swimming pool, it was far ahead of its time. Charlie Noble used the swimming pool at early morning hours, but because of the damaging effect of steam and moisture on furniture, doors, and all woodwork, the pioneer pool had to be removed.

He was considerate of his hired help and popular with his neighbors. His compassion was genuine, and he reeled at the sight of horses suffering from overwork or shortage of feed. It was neither accurate nor just to say that he lacked sentiment.

Like an introvert artist with watercolors, he obtained fun in seeing dreams coming true, not on canvas but in big wheat fields and agricultural improvement. The great enthusiasm of which he was capable seemed to be born in satisfaction with what he was doing. It was an enthusiasm that refused to be diminished. If anything was needed to revive enthusiasm for his work in this eighty-year-old man, the expanding Noble factory and the good reports he was getting about the Noble Blade Cultivator were enough to supply it. A letter written from Clovis, New Mexico, to his wife on April 3, 1953, radiated with zest for what he was doing:

"Dear Maggie," he wrote. "This is the most fertile field I have ever seen for our machines, and, my, how they do need a soil Doctor. There is no end to the very important work to be done . . . ." Travelling as he was on a promotion tour in that southern region, he was thinking, no doubt, that if he were thirty years of age instead of eighty, he would enjoy nothing more than to settle down and be a soil doctor or soil missionary where he could do the most good.

He was a generous supporter of the church, the Red Cross, the YMCA, and any other worthy organization. His contributions were made quietly, inconspicuously. He didn't talk about flowers and trees but he liked them, and at his own expense, in June, 1919, he hired an expert horticulturist, A. Mitchell, to move into the village and make Nobleford "the prettiest spot in Alberta."[5]

Those people who worked for Charlie Noble and were thus in the best position to judge were the first to say that he was an honest man. The person who bought a horse that was found later to have stringhalt was invited to bring the animal back and accept the return of his purchase money. The man whose two horses bought from Noble were later killed by lightning was surprised to find them being replaced by the seller. When Mr. Noble sat as a director of an independent grain company and heard that a certain elevator agent in the company's service was being recommended for a bonus because the man had shown substantial "overage," Noble protested and resigned from the directorship forthwith.

On only one known occasion was he suspected of theft, and when the facts became known, everybody, including Noble, found it more laughable than serious. It was at Gymon, Oklahoma, when Mr. Noble was on a farm machinery promotion tour, driving his Chrysler car with a trailer hitch. After having lunch, he was about to leave the town, and upon emerging from the restaurant, he entered his car, backed up a few feet to get the needed clearance for driving forward, and pulled away.

Before going far, he noticed a half ton truck travelling closely behind him — too close for safe driving — and he pulled over to let the offending small truck go past. But the truck did not pass. Instead, it remained close behind the Chrysler, and the Canadian, feeling annoyed with the other driver who appeared to be playing tricks, slowed down to determine the reason for the indignity. But at this point, a police car with lights flashing bore down upon him from the rear. Noble obeyed the police signal and pulled to the curb and stopped.

The officer inspected Noble's license and asked accusingly where he was going with the stolen half ton truck and if he thought he could get away with it as far as Canada. Only then did Charlie Noble realize that when he moved his car in reverse after leaving the restaurant, his trailer hitch had hooked into the bumper of the truck parked behind him, and unwittingly he had driven away with another person's truck.

To a spectator, the circumstances would have looked exactly like those of car theft, but when the Canadian laughed at the ridiculous situation, the Oklahoma policeman did the same, and the embarrassed Noble was able to go on his way, his reputation for honest dealings still untarnished.

He made his mistakes and some of them were costly, but nobody questioned the moral purposes that ruled his life. Even that lifelong preoccupation with conservation was rooted in moral principles. His own statements furnished the proof, for example: "It is the next generation that pays for the sins of careless or greedy soil management. The man who would earn the full respect of his son should make sure the young man inherits the soil as well as the farm." They were the words of a philosopher. They were the words of a good citizen, and happily, his good citizenship did not go unnoticed. High honors came to Charles Sherwood Noble, bringing high honors to the prairie soil as well as to the man.

When the Royal Honors List was published from London in 1943, on it were the names of three distinguished men of agriculture from western Canada — Charles Noble of Nobleford and his friends Dr. W. H. Fairfield of Lethbridge and Seager Wheeler of Rosthern, Saskatchewan. The citation in each case said: "For valuable service to agriculture." The award was the coveted "Member of the Order of the British Empire."

A few years later, 1951, when the Alberta Agricultural Hall of Fame was opened with the hanging of the first group of portraits of distinguished farmers, the name and picture of Charles Noble were among them, and visitors at the ceremony heard the words of praise that: "No one has done more for soil conservation in Alberta than Charles S. Noble. His early perception of the problems involved and his constant search for a solution have resulted in his recognition as one of our outstanding soil conservationists. In spite of adversity and early criticism of his ideas, his faith in the outcome continued undiminished."

A year later, 1952, Charles Noble was honored by the University of Alberta with an award of an honorary degree. Dean A. G. McCalla, in presenting the candidate, concluded by saying: "It can seldom be said of any man that he has changed the face of the land, and have it taken literally. It can be so said of Mr. Noble. Eminent Chancellor, I have the honor to present to you for the degree of Doctor of Laws Honoris Causa, Charles Sherwood Noble."

Nor was that all. In October, 1951, the famous farmer was installed as an honorary life member of the Lethbridge Chamber of Commerce, and just days before his death in 1957, Dr. Noble was awarded an honorary life membership in the Agricultural Institute of Canada.

They were great occasions, bringing joy to friends and members of the Noble family, but one of the happiest events of that period was on June 30, 1953, four years before Dr. Noble's death and fifty years to the day after Charles S. Noble and Margaret Fraser were married in Calgary, when the famous couple celebrated their golden wedding anniversary. What made it unique was the expression of gratitude that life had become steadily richer to make this the happiest day of their lives. It was good to know that it could be that way.

Mother Noble died on December 20, 1955, and Dr. Charles, described as "Alberta's most famous farmer-inventor," died on July 5, 1957. The tributes were legion, many of them expressing a similar sentiment: "With the death of C. S. Noble, Alberta loses the one man who above all others led the way to more productive farming methods under Alberta weather and soil conditions."[6]

To make prairie farms more productive was what he aimed to do, that and to leave the soil undamaged for the farmers and their bread-eating fellows in the next generation, and the next and the next.

NOTES

1 A Nut about Prairie Soils

1. Notice of Dry Farming Meetings to be addressed by H. W. Campbell, *Farm and Ranch Review.* Authorized by Prov. Dept. of Agriculture, June, 1907.
2. Hon. Duncan Marshall, "Dry Farming Adventures," *Family Herald and Weekly Star,* Oct. 15, 1941.
3. Angus MacKay, "Origin of Summerfallow," *Farm and Ranch Review,* Jan. 6, 1913.
4. H. W. Campbell, "Lecture on Dry Farming," *Farm and Ranch Review,* July, 1907.
5. Asael E. Palmer, *When the Winds Came,* Lethbridge, privately printed, n.d.
6. F. L. Duley (research supervisor, U.S.D.A. Soil and Water Conservation Research, College of Agriculture, Lincoln, Nebraska) to O. S. Longman, June 25, 1956.

2 Charlie Will Make His Mark in the World

1. Newell James Noble, "Charles Sherwood Noble," Noble papers in the possession of Shirley F. Noble, c. 1915.

3 Soil and Scenery in the Canadian Foothills

1. Claresholm History Book Club, *Where the Wheatlands Meet the Range,* Claresholm, 1974, p. 7.
2. The McKinney section of land was 17-12-26-W of 4, three miles southeast of Claresholm.
3. S. F. Noble, "Noble Sowed New Ideas," *Lethbridge Herald,* Dec. 28, 1967.

4. Claresholm News Column, *Macleod Gazette,* June 5, 1903.
5. The homestead quarter was the N.W. of 32-12-27-W of 4.
6. Claresholm News Column, *Macleod Gazette,* June 12, 1903.
7. Ibid., July 10, 1903.
8. Claresholm Club, *Wheatlands,* p. 35.
9. Claresholm News Column, *Macleod Gazette,* Dec. 15, 1904.
10. *Nanton News,* Dec. 15, 1904.
11. Claresholm Club, *Wheatlands,* p. 35.
12. *Nanton News,* Sept. 28, 1905.

4 Born to Be Busy

1. Claresholm News Column, *Macleod Gazette,* July 10, 1903.
2. Ibid., Jan. 8, 1904.
3. Ibid., Feb. 5, 1904.
4. William Cochrane, memo concerning the first year in Canada, William Cochrane papers in the possession of T. R. Cochrane, Calgary.
5. *Claresholm Review,* Apr. 1, 1909.
6. Ibid., July 31, 1908.
7. Ibid., Nov. 4, 1909.
8. Ibid., Apr. 29, 1909.
9. Ibid., Mar. 20, 1908.

5 Milnes and Noble—Real Estate and Other Lines

1. C. S. Noble, letter written in Denver, Colorado, to son S. F. Noble, Jan. 3, 1947.
2. "A Dizzy Little Town," *Manitoba Free Press,* Sept. 28, 1907. Reprinted by *Claresholm Review,* Oct. 4, 1907.
3. *Claresholm Review,* Aug. 19, 1909.
4. Ibid., Apr. 1, 1909.
5. Ibid., Apr. 15, 1909.
6. Ibid., Apr. 29, 1909.
7. Ibid., Mar. 13, 1908.

6 To a Place Called Noble

1. *Claresholm Review,* Aug. 19, 1909.
2. Ibid., May 31, 1907.
3. Ibid., May 24, 1907.
4. Ibid., Sept. 16, 1909.
5. C.P.R. Land Sales, Vol. 49, 1909, Glenbow-Alberta Archives, Calgary.
6. Ibid.

7. *Claresholm Review,* May 6, 1909.
8. C.P.R. Land Sales, Vol. 49, 1909, Glenbow-Alberta Archives.
9. *Lethbridge Herald,* Sept. 20, 1909.
10. *Claresholm Review,* Dec. 23, 1909.
11. *Lethbridge Herald,* Nov. 1, 1909.

7 The Spirit of Dry Farming, 1912

1. *Lethbridge Herald,* Sept. 16, 1911.
2. Ibid., Aug. 30, 1910.
3. Ibid., Oct. 21, 1912.
4. *Farm and Ranch Review,* Nov. 20, 1912.
5. Ibid.

8 The Noble Foundation

1. *Farm and Ranch Review,* Nov. 20, 1913.
2. Ibid.
3. Leonard Nesbitt, *Brooks Bulletin,* Sept. 22, 1966.
4. S. F. Noble to O. S. Longman, June 14, 1956, copy at Glenbow-Alberta Archives.
5. Noble Foundation Prospectus, 1913.
6. Noble Foundation Report, 1918.

9 Patriotism and Production

1. Hon. Martin Burrell, *Lethbridge Herald,* Jan. 29, 1915.
2. *Lethbridge Herald,* Feb. 10, 1915.
3. Ibid., June 8, 1915.
4. C. S. Noble, "Strong Appeal for Greater Production," *Lethbridge Herald,* Mar. 8, 1915.
5. Ibid.
6. *Lethbridge Herald,* Apr. 19, 1916.
7. Cora Hind, *Winnipeg Free Press,* Aug. 26, 1916.
8. *Lethbridge Herald,* Oct. 25, 1916.
9. Ibid., Oct. 26, 1916.

10 Food Will Win the War

1. *Lethbridge Herald,* Oct. 20, 1917.
2. Ibid., June 14, 1918.
3. Ibid., Feb. 3, 1919.
4. Ibid., Mar. 9, 1918.
5. Ibid., Apr. 18, 1918.

6. O. S. Longman, notes in the Charles Noble files, Glenbow-Alberta Archives.
7. T. Childs, *Canadian Cattlemen,* May 19, 1955, p. 25.
8. Anne Tiffany, memo to O. S. Longman, Glenbow-Alberta Archives.
9. S. F. Noble, article on Charles Noble, a copy of which was given to the author of the present work.
10. *Lethbridge Herald,* Aug. 23, 1917.
11. Ibid., June 30, 1917.
12. Ibid., Mar. 30, 1918.
13. Ibid., Mar. 1, 1919.

11 Postwar Worries

1. *Lethbridge Herald,* Mar. 18, 1919.
2. Ibid., Feb. 27, 1920.
3. Ibid., June 16, 1919.
4. *Alberta Gazette,* June 14, 1919, p. 353.
5. *Lethbridge Herald,* May 4, 1920.
6. Ibid., May 6, 1920.
7. Ibid., June 19, 1920.
8. Ibid., June 29, 1920.
9. Ibid., June 19, 1920.
10. Ibid., Oct. 1, 1920.

12 Historic Harvest Scenes at the Cameron, 1920

1. *Lethbridge Herald,* Aug. 19, 1920.
2. Ibid., Aug. 2, 1920.
3. *Calgary Herald,* Aug. 19, 1920.
4. Ibid.
5. Robert Gratz, interview conducted by O. S. Longman, July 30, 1957, Charles Noble files, Glenbow-Alberta Archives.
6. Lillian Noble, "The Noble Story," Nobleford and Monarch History Book Club, *Sons of Wind and Soil* (Calgary: D. W. Friesen and Son, Ltd., 1976), p. 300.
7. *Lethbridge Herald,* Sept. 16, 1920.

13 The Power Struggle in the Noble Fields

1. J. E. Slater to the *Farmer's Advocate,* Nov. 16, 1910, p. 1631.
2. C. S. Noble, "Horse and Tractor," *Grain Growers' Guide,* June 16, 1920.
3. Ibid.
4. Elmer A. Updike to editor, *Farm and Ranch Review,* Oct. 5, 1921.

14 When the Walls Came Tumbling Down

1. Saskatchewan Grain Growers' Association, *Annual Report,* Feb., 1922.
2. C. S. Noble, *Financial Post,* Jan. 20, 1922.
3. *Calgary Herald,* May 13, 1921.
4. *Lethbridge Herald,* May 13, 1921.
5. James Murray to O. S. Longman, June 22, 1956, Glenbow-Alberta Archives.
6. *Lethbridge Herald,* Feb. 18, 1921.
7. Ibid., Feb. 22, 1921.
8. Ibid., Feb. 26, 1921.
9. C. S. Noble, *Financial Post,* Jan. 20, 1922.
10. C. S. Noble, letter written in Denver, Colorado, to son S. F. Noble, Jan. 3, 1947.
11. C. S. Noble to Hon. George Hoadley, Dec. 21, 1922, Noble file, Glenbow-Alberta Archives.
12. *Calgary Herald,* Mar. 6, 1923.
13. Ibid., Mar. 12, 1923.
14. O. S. Longman, list of lands transferred at foreclosure, Longman compilation, Oct. 10, 1957, Glenbow-Alberta Archives.
15. *Calgary Herald,* Apr. 13, 1923.
16. S. F. Noble, "Dr. Charles S. Noble," *When the Winds Came,* Asael Palmer, n.d.
17. C. S. Noble to Hon. George Hoadley, Dec. 21, 1922, Noble file, Glenbow-Alberta Archives.

15 Rebuilding the Wall

1. S. F. Noble, "Noble Sowed New Ideas," *Lethbridge Herald,* Dec. 28, 1967.
2. *Lethbridge Herald,* May 12, 1923.
3. C. S. Noble, ibid., Aug. 13, 1926.
4. Ibid., July 16, 1925.
5. *Lethbridge Herald,* Aug. 22, 1925.
6. Lillian Noble, "The Noble Story."
7. Hon. Duncan Marshall, "Dry Farming Adventures," *Family Herald and Weekly Star,* Oct. 15, 1941.

16 The Great Parade of Combines

1. *Lethbridge Herald,* Jan. 26, 1916.
2. Ibid., Oct. 25, 1912.
3. Ibid., Sept. 24, 1927.
4. Ibid., Nov. 24, 1927.
5. Ibid., Jan. 14, 1929.

6. Ibid., Aug. 17, 1929.
7. Ibid., Aug. 3, 1929.

17 Drifting Soil and Its Evil Companions

1. P. M. Abel, "Soil Drifting," *Grain Growers' Guide,* July 28, 1920.
2. L. P. Tuff, "Soil Drifting," *Lethbridge Herald,* Aug. 7, 1915.
3. *Lethbridge Herald,* Apr. 12, 1921.
4. Ibid., Aug. 13, 1921.
5. Herbert Chester, "The Development of Soil Drifting Control," seminar paper presented in Lethbridge, Mar. 5, 1953.
6. *Lethbridge Herald,* July 2, 1932.
7. C. S. Noble, "Farmers Urged to Adopt New and Better Methods to Prevent Soil Drifting," ibid., June 19, 1920.
8. Hon. Duncan Marshall, "Dry Farming Adventures," *Family Herald and Weekly Star,* Oct. 15, 1941.

18 The Noble Blade

1. *Lethbridge Herald,* Mar. 16, 1932.
2. Ibid., May 11, 1934.
3. C. W. Peterson, *Farm and Ranch Review,* July 5, 1921.
4. O. S. Longman, notes from interviews with C. S. Noble, Glenbow-Alberta Archives.
5. *Lethbridge Herald,* Aug. 16, 1935.
6. Ibid., June 3, 1937.
7. Ibid., July 31, 1937.
8. S. F. Noble, "Black Blizzards," ibid., Feb. 23, 1952.
9. S. F. Noble, "Dr. Charles S. Noble," *When the Winds Came,* Asael Palmer, n.d.
10. Leonard Nesbitt, *Brooks Bulletin,* Sept. 9, 1966.

19 Animal Husbandman

1. *Farm and Ranch Review,* Nov. 20, 1913.
2. James Murray to O. S. Longman, June 28, 1956.
3. Wilma Flitton, interview, Calgary, Jan. 13, 1980.
4. *Alberta Brand Book,* 1921-1924.
5. *Lethbridge Herald,* Apr. 26, 1934.
6. Ibid., Dec. 7, 1956.

20 After Fifty Years

1. Ecclesiastes 9:10.

21 The Measure of the Man

1. C. W. Peterson, *Farm and Ranch Review,* July 15, 1921.
2. Wilma Flitton, notes furnished Jan. 15, 1980.
3. F. L. Duley to O. S. Longman, June 25, 1956.
4. *Lethbridge Herald,* Dec. 29, 1917.
5. Ibid., June 10, 1919.
6. R. L. King, "C. S. Noble is Worth Remembering," *Camrose Canadian,* Aug. 13, 1957.

INDEX

Massey Harris combines, 144, 148
Mather, H. J., 168
Mathews, D. G., 8, 159
Merchants Bank, 80, 127
Milnes, T. C., 36; and C. S. Noble, 34, 38, 42, 45, 48
Moffat, William, 25, 43
Monarch, Alta., 47, 155
Monarch-Nobleford district, 157, 158, 160
Motherwell, W. R., 30, 52
Mountain View Farm, 46, 49, 68
Mules, 33, 173
Murray, James, 64, 107, 119, 128, 156, 177

Nesbitt, Leonard, 62, 171
Noble, Alta., 43, 47
Noble and Harris Land Co., 111
Noble blade, 8, 160, 171, 180
Noble Cultivators Ltd., 170
Noble Farms, Ltd., 142
Nobleford, Alta., 46, 75
Noble Foundation, 60, 65, 89, 90, 105, 111
Noble Foundation General Store, 80, 87
Noble, Alleen, 142
Noble, Gerald, 108, 179
Noble, Hubert and Jemima, 10
Noble, Lillian, 114
Noble, Margaret, 43
Noble, Newell James, 65, 87, 165, 189
Noble, Shirley F., 23, 86, 108, 137, 169, 179, 181, 182, 184
Noble, Will, 22
Noble, William, 11, 17

Old Man River, 111, 113
Oxen, 31
Oxley Ranch, 20

Palmer, Asael, 7, 8, 159, 160
Perry, A., 56
Peterson, C. W., 187
Pigs, 174

Plowless summerfallow, 162, 169
Prairie Farm Rehabilitation Act, 158, 188
Prairie Grange Farm, 68

Qu'Appelle Valley Farming Co., 63

Receivership, 127
Reeves steam tractor, 34, 49, 88, 89, 112
Rosen rye, 190
Rossiter, E. J., 90
Rumely Oil Pull tractor, 56
Russell, J. C., 169, 188
Rye, 110

Sedgwick, Parker, 11
Sedgwick, Tryphena, 11
Seed drill inventions, 140
Sherman, Andy, 124, 172
Sherwood, Henry, 41
Sherwood, Jemima, 10
Shuttleworth, A. E., 74
Soil depletion, 4
Soil erosion, 4, 72
Soil survey, 126, 150
Stanley wheat, 57
Steam tractors, 14, 34, 64, 89, 119, 120
Stevens, W. J., 84
Stewart stock loader, 112
Strip farming, 153, 161
Summerfallow, 7, 107

Taggart, Gordon, 8
Taitenger, Nick, 40
Thomson, L. B., 8, 159
Trash cover, 8, 158, 163
Trego, W. D., 157
Tuff, L. P., 155

United Farmers of Alberta, 102, 126
United States Soil Conservation Service, 169
University of Alberta, 73
University of Saskatchewan, 73